Green Bank

Driving Across America in Search of a Promised Land

By Kedem Spears

Second Edition

To my mom and dad, who fostered a love of culture and traveling in me, and who were willing to financially support me all these years

To my friends, the ones who enjoy spending time with me and who accept me as I am in a society that is not always very accepting

To the people of Manhattan Beach, California, for being my friends all these years

To the electrosensitives of Green Bank, West Virginia, for their perseverance in their avoidance of and their fight against the electromagnetic radiation some people are so sensitive to

Table of Contents

I.	How I found out about Green Bank	4
II.	Heading Out	17
III.	Middle America	27
IV.	West Virginia	37
V.	With my Aunt	50
VI.	Philadelphia Heading West	61
VII.	The South	68
VIII.	The West	88
IX.	Back in Southern California	101
X.	To West Virginia, Again	104
XI.	Back in the WV	119
XII.	East, then West	135
XIII.	The River Cities	142
XIV.	Back Out West	154
	Epilogue	164

I.   How I found out about Green Bank

I am a native Angeleno, born and raised in that large city on the edge of the continent. Los Angeles can be paradise. The weather is pleasant almost all year round, the scenery is fantastic, the people are beautiful, and there is a lot to do. Most people who move there do not want to move anywhere else. That is why I also loved that place. Save for vacations I took elsewhere, the big city was all I knew. Moving to the country seemed too foreign to me, but once I got older that began to change, and like many native Angelenos I was thinking of leaving. The people were not the most friendly, it was too expensive, and when I wanted to move out of my parents' place, I could not afford it. Also, the people were hooked to their cell phones.

I am electrosensitive, so the radiation from cell phones was always a problem for me since my mother first got one. I noticed that when I put that device to my ear it caused it to scratch and I would start getting brain fog. I would experience that symptom and headaches even if I was within a few feet of others using their cell phones. For a long time, I could easily avoid being around other people on their phones and not be exposed to this radiation. All I had to do was ask my friends not to use their phones near me and hope they would be understanding. By the early 2010s, however, this was no longer practical. Wi-fi (which uses the same type of signals as cell phones) had become ubiquitous and smartphones were just coming into wide use.

I was going to graduate school at that time. I was studying Public Administration and Urban Planning, wanting to help solve the traffic problems in Southern California among other things. However, I found it difficult sit in class. At least ten students in the room would be using their wi-fi to surf the Internet and they would not always listen when I asked them not to sit near me. As such, I would regularly feel as if electric signals were going through my brain. Eventually, unless it was a teacher with a very strict anti electronics policy, I had to stop coming to class and leave a recording device so that I could listen to the lecture. And it was not only in school. Other places where I went to see friends became off limits as I was surrounded by people going on their smartphones. I could no longer go to concerts, crowded events, or anywhere where there was a long line. I had to start socially distancing long before there was any Covid pandemic.

Electrosensitivity, or more properly electrohypersensitivity (EHS) is a controversial diagnosis. Cell phones have not been around long enough for studies to show irrefutable evidence of their harm or that some people are more sensitive to them than others. However, much of this is because of the influence phone and technology companies have. Whenever they make studies, they make them in such a way to show their devices are not harmful, and a general public who is addicted to their devices tend to believe them. This is not very different from what the tobacco and oil industries used to do about their products before there was irrefutable evidence of their harm. Already most independent studies show cell phones and other wireless technology do have a potential for harm, and just like some people are more allergic to peanuts or sunlight than others, there are obviously some people who are more allergic to electromagnetic radiation. But because the public still has doubts over this issue, many people refuse to accept my sensitivities and tell me that it is just psychological.

One day in 2011 while my mother was watching the Israeli TV she found something that could help me. I was still living with my parents at that time, and my mother would regularly ask me to watch things on the Israeli TV, which I resisted. I did not want to be immersed in my ethnic heritage all the time and my mother would often call me to watch things with her right when I wanted to do something else, such as now when I came back home two hours before dinner to take a nap. However, now when my mother told me the clip was about my sensitivity to wi-fi, I agreed to watch it.

The deep voiced anchor was talking about the condition I had. He said he used his cell phone all the time and did not experience negative symptoms, but also acknowledged that cell phones had not been around long enough to know their long term effects. Then he said there was a 13000 square mile place in the United States called the National Radio Quiet Zone where wireless signals were limited. The zone was centered around the town of Green Bank, West Virginia, home to the National Radio Astronomy Observatory, as to allow the telescopes to receive faint radio and microwave signals from outer space without interference. As such, for ten miles around Green Bank, cell phones and wi-fi were completely banned. Dozens of people who were sensitive to cell phones were moving there.

My mother suggested we go to Green Bank to check it out. I thought the mountains near there would be a good place to start a bed and breakfast or a restaurant and to interact with people away from their cell phones. However, I had reservations. It was far from where I lived in Los Angeles. It was in West Virginia, one of the worst reputed states in the country, a place I imagined was full of closed minded rednecks. The people on the show expressed emotional difficulties of moving to Green Bank. One woman was quite bitter about leaving behind all her friends in Maine. If moving from a rural part of Maine was so hard for her, how difficult would it be for me to move from the big city where I lived my whole life all the way across the country to West Virginia.

For me it was not only EHS, it was also the autism spectrum. I have Asperger's, and as such I am not built quite like a typical person. I am not someone to marry, settle down, and have kids. I do not have the social skills for marriage and I never liked little kids. I cannot even get into romantic relationships, as much as I had tried in the past. As such, being a person who still needs friends, I befriend people in unusual ways. Living in Los Angeles by the airport, I would regularly go seven miles down to Manhattan Beach and hang out with the people working at the boutiques there, or make friends with the locals at the beach who had friends at the stores. Manhattan Beach for me was like the high school and college community I was no longer part of but that in absence of a steady relationship or a family of my own I still needed.

Then there were the various sensitivities and dislikes I had, in addition to cell phones. These included sweating, bees, noise, and dogs, among other things. Dogs was the biggest issue for people with me, besides cell phones and wi-fi. Nearly all my life I had been afraid of dogs. I am not too concerned about them biting, as owners almost always have that under control, but I am concerned about the licking. I never wanted a dog to lick me, as it is still the dog getting its mouth on me. However, in a society that is increasingly dog friendly, this was not something everyone was willing to understand.

There were many who did not accept me for my unique ways. I was regularly criticized for the way I was making friends, which given the difficulty I already had with that merely added insult to injury. As for dogs, whenever I asked people to get them out of my way, they would retort with "he's friendly". People also told me I should learn to accept dogs licking me and that I should go to therapy for that. However, I was someone proud of my Asperger's who did not want to change out of it, just like a gay person or a Jew does not want to change out of it. Unfortunately, we are not at the point of accepting Aspergerics or people with neurological differences as they are. Even my mother was not always someone to accept me as I was. As such, I needed to move out of my parents after having lived with them thirty years. To answer my need for acceptance I had to move not only somewhere where cell phone use was low, but that was also very liberal.

After finishing graduate school in 2012, I began my explorations. First I went to the San Francisco Bay Area, arguably the most liberal place in the United States. I did not know how it would be with cell phones, however, as it was still an urban area. San Francisco proper did have heavy cell phone use, and I could not go to the crowded restaurants my friends wanted to go to. I did not even bother looking at Silicon Valley, as I knew what technology use would be like over there. The suburbs did have a lot of cell phone use, though when I came back to L.A. I noticed that the use in the San Francisco suburbs was a bit less than in L.A. I drove up the coast all the way to Eureka to see what it was like in the smaller towns and rural areas. Cell phone use remained fairly heavy in all these places. In Eureka, my waiter told me that nearly all his friends had smartphones. The one area where I did not see a lot of cell phone use was in Mendocino and Fort Bragg. It was a super liberal area and one that almost never got hotter than 70 degrees, a boon for a heat sensitive person like me. However, the people there also seemed very scruffy. I had to move on.

Some people suggested I move to Portland, so on my next trip I went there and to other places in the Northwest. Portland was still the big city, but since it was a very liberal, artsy, and nature oriented one, I figured cell phone use would not be too heavy over there, and I was right. I went to Seattle to visit the family I had there and to check out some nearby places. Seattle, as might be expected for a tech center, did have heavy cell phone use. With its traffic, high cost of living, and large size, the whole city was like Los Angeles but with more rain. I went with my dad to the San Juan Islands, specifically the sparsely populated Lopez Island. The island had one tiny town with a building that served both as the restaurant and post office. There was only one other person sitting at a table, and low and behold, she was staring at her smartphone. I found it surprising that a device had not even existed a few years earlier had made its way to one of the most remote corners of the lower 48 states. I also checked out Port Townsend, a town of 9000 people with a cohousing community that attracted me. It was a charming place, very Victorian era and built with the intention of becoming a large city before Seattle outbid it. However, it was not for me. Nearly all the residents were old, and the few young people were more interested in being on their screens than in talking to others.

I decided Portland would be the place for me. I found a couple apartments there I liked and that were nice but not too expensive. But then, right on the day my parents were going to get their plane tickets to help with my move, I was at an event at my university when a student from Olympia, Washington told me I should check that place out and that it would be better than Portland (her mother became the mayor of Olympia a year later). As soon as she told me that, I called my parents and told them to hold off on the plane ticket. Now I went on my own both to Portland and to Olympia to check them out, and added a couple more places I was considering. I did not like Olympia too much- it was way too grungy. Portland also seemed a bit too grungy now. In addition, the stores were too busy for me to hang out and the town was super dog friendly. The suburbs of Portland were not grungy, but neither were they too liberal and the people there were on their cell phones just as much as everywhere else. I decided the smaller Eugene would be a happy medium and that was where I ended up moving.

Eugene had its aging hippies, college students, hipsters, and Middle American families, all of when lived within this city that was only a few miles across and with its neighborhoods integrated with one another. In sum, it was a very diverse place, even if it was mostly just a diversity of white people. The people got along with one another except for when it came to radical leftists that not everyone agreed with. This was a place where if you did not like dogs or little kids, people accepted it without trying to change you (even if the town was very dog friendly). People who moved there from more conservative places all told me people were more accepting of them in Eugene than where they came from.

However, the people there were not too friendly. A few people liked seeing me at the stores, but when it came to friending them on social media, getting lunch with them, or anything beyond just occasionally conversing with them, they wanted nothing to do with me. Others did not even want to talk to me in the stores. They were nice to me one day but the next day they shrugged me off. I also missed my parents, whom I had never lived away from. As much as I did not want to go back to living with them, I did not want to be in a different city from them either. After two months in Eugene, I had enough and decided I would come back to L.A. and look for an apartment there.

When I came back to L.A. I was back with my parents who were not always completely accepting of me. I tried looking for my own apartment, but where I could afford a nice one for 1000 a month in Eugene I could not find a good quality one for 1500 in Los Angeles. So after four months I went back to Eugene. The only reasons I lasted there this time as long as I did were that I did not want to move back in with my parents and that cell phone use in Eugene was indeed relatively low. Even in 2014, many people still only had flip phones there, and one of my friends was proud of having that instead of a smartphone. Another one talked to me for an hour without ever staring at her phone and I could not remember when that was last the case for me in Southern California. Even if there was some background radiation in Eugene, I could easily drive into the forests nearby where the radiation was almost nil. There the restorative air cleared me of any brain fog or migraines I may have had and my mind freely roamed thinking about life and various things I wanted to write.

Then a year after moving, some of my friends in Eugene had turned against me and I decided it was time for me to come back to Southern California. I realized that just because people are liberal does not mean they are kind. On the contrary, many people who greatly value their freedom also believe they can be as mean as they want and that they do not owe anyone anything. And frankly, many people in Eugene are not liberal, but instead of arguing with you, they simply shrug you off, because that is the more acceptable thing to do there. I also later on read that Oregon is supposedly one of the five most introverted states in the United States. That is good if you want solitude and people who will not judge you, but not if you want friends.

When I moved back to Southern California, I still could not afford Los Angeles, so I moved to the town of Oxnard sixty miles up the coast from Downtown L.A. in the metropolitan area's exurban fringes. It was not as bad of a place as reputation sometimes gives it. My college friend Stasia lived there. It was by the beach and had the same pleasant weather as the Los Angeles Westside where I grew up. My beloved Manhattan Beach was an hour and a half away, but I still went there nearly every day. And my drive was not too bad. I had Pacific Coast Highway as a direct route, a road that not only afforded dramatic ocean views, but also passed outside the most crowded parts of the metropolitan area and thus meant relatively light traffic. My day could start off in a depressed mood, but whenever I went to Manhattan Beach in the afternoon and saw the people I liked, my day became so much brighter. It felt that that was what I was living for.

Moving back to Southern California was not all it was cut out to be, however. I was back in a place with heavy cell phone use. I was back in a place where people were not accepting of my avoidance of dogs. I was 37 years old in 2019, and by then the good friends I had in college were all married or living out of town. The one exception was Stasia, but she was not someone I always got along with. I had my friends in Manhattan Beach, but finding good and genuine friends could be very difficult. The worst for me was when people would cancel on me, and this was now happening to me all the time. My friends and I would plan to have lunch or dinner. I would get very excited about going to eat with them, but then at the last minute they canceled. They would not always even message me in a timely manner and in those cases I would drive nearly two hours to see them, often through traffic and not always on the days it was most convenient for me, only to learn once I got there that they would not show up. Whenever that happened, I got very hurt, no matter how much I got used to it.

Some people suggested I change my social scene and join organizations. I already did that- I was a part of Mensa- but I did not form strong connections with the members. Society is built so that people my age will marry or have long term relationships. Some people did ask me why would I not try to do that and have someone to be with me for the rest of our lives. If I would find the right person, that would be nice, but for me it is not very realistic, despite the optimism shows like *Love on the Spectrum* try to show. Marriage involves what I call the C word- compromise- which can be very difficult for people with Asperger's. I am fine with compromising on small things, but marriage involves compromising on very big things, and often changing your life for someone else. Most women want to have children, which I absolutely do not want. I am not going to run after noisy and messy little kids because that is what my wife will want. My mother tried telling me that many women nowadays do not want to have children. That is true, but those who do not want children want dogs.

I also did not have a job. I worked for a year as a construction estimator before I was laid off in 2008 right before the Great Recession. I tried finding other jobs, but besides a few tutoring gigs that lasted no more than one session, no one would hire me. Organizations offering job assistance for people with special needs do not focus on high functioning people and they tried offering me more menial jobs that I would not take. And even if I would find a good job, they would likely want me to have a cell phone that I would use, and make little or no accommodations for my electrosensitivity. Eventually I decided I would stop looking for jobs and focus on being a writer.

I spent three years writing a book about my life and my experiences growing up with Asperger's, a book that totaled 355 pages. But right as I was finishing editing it, cancel culture was in full swing. Woke and cancel culture listen to the voices of some people, but not too much to those with neurological differences, and not even too much to the disabled in general. When one has a neurological difference and sees the world in a way that does not agree with the views of groups of disenfranchised people who are abled, one is bound to get canceled, trolled, given a bad reputation, etc. I did not want to have to choose between telling a compromised version of my life story and telling a complete one but facing trolls and negative media attention, so that thing I worked so hard on I had to leave unpublished.

* * *

I have always liked traveling. When I was a child, I would often go with my parents on short vacations to places like Santa Barbara or San Diego. I also took trips to Israel every few years to visit family over there. Once I became a teenager I came to appreciate different places more, leading my parents and I to travel to a greater variety of places both domestically and abroad. When I was in college, I decided to make tourism my major. My parents and I went on many trips together into my adult years. We went to Morocco to see the country where my father was born before moving to Israel. We went on multiple cruises, visiting the Caribbean and sailing through the Panama Canal. We took another cruise around the Baltic to Russia. We also went on a cruise around Italy and Greece on the sister ship of the one that got wrecked in that area in 2012 only two weeks before that happened. In total, we traveled to 33 countries.

That Italy cruise was the last overseas trip I took. It was at that time that airplanes were increasingly adding wi-fi. I always liked that cell phones were not allowed on airplanes, as the radiation on planes is especially severe. For one thing, you are closer to the people using their devices. Also, because an airplane is a metallic structure, the radiation bounces off the walls and thus gets amplified. That is why I feel the radiation more in cars and elevators also. And this is not mentioning the cosmic radiation found at the high altitudes planes fly at. So when wi-fi became introduced on airplanes and came into wide use, I stopped flying.

I never stopped liking to travel, however. I just now did that in my car. And I did stop liking to travel with others. My parents did not always get along with each other and when you threw them into a trip and added me to the mix, things could become worse. I started traveling with my friends for some time, but being in tight quarters with them for multiple days, I did not always get along with them either. These were friends who wanted to go shopping instead of visiting the sites like I did. They would want to stay up and go to the bars when I wanted to sleep at a decent time. One time my friend would not pay her share of the cost, and it was not until I asked her friend to talk to her that she agreed to pay up. I decided that unless I had a very easy going friend who can take multiple days off, the best was for me to travel would be on my own. I would visit friends who lived on the way or at my destination, but the rest of the time I would be on my own.

After I moved back to Oxnard, I took several such trips to explore places I wanted to move to in the western states. My parents were never too happy about me taking these trips on my own, and kept asking me to take them along. They tried telling me that they would try not to argue, and they would downplay the arguments we were bound to have and emphasize how much they enjoyed the places I took them to and told me that that outweighed the bad times. However, the traumas I incurred from our intense arguments did sometimes outweigh the enjoyment and I could not travel with them anymore. I honestly still do want to travel with my parents once again before they die and while they are in relatively good health, but I find it very difficult to talk to them about not arguing with me. Furthermore, my parents can't change who they are just like I can't change who I am. My dad cannot stop being bad tempered and my mom, as a mother, cannot hold herself back from being frustrated at some of my ways when she is with me for a long time. For people not on the spectrum who are more like everyone else and have successful jobs, they no longer have a reason to not get along with their parents as adults. For those of us who are different, however, that is not the case.

When visiting the various towns and cities on the trips I took on my own- Santa Fe, Denver, Boulder, Durango, among others, it was difficult to tell what type of relationships I would have there. In all these places there were nice people, but what if the place I chose would be another Oregon and people would only be nice to me the first few days? I also looked at various intentional communities, knowing that at these places I would have an immediate community. However, many of them had too many unusual rules and did not value individual freedom too much. Dancing Rabbit, a well known place some people suggested to me, for example, did not allow people to have their own cars. There were some less restrictive ones, but even in those ones the houses were not of a very good quality, the people lived a bit too simply for my standards, and they were not always most accommodating to people with disabilities. Except for the most restrictive or off the grid communities, people would be tied to their cell phones, and there would be community members with dogs. After being at a loss over where to live and being increasingly depressed in Southern California, Stasia and I had a talk and we decided the best place for me to move to and the one where I would be truly happy was Green Bank, West Virginia.

* * *

When I was twelve, I first watched *Rain Man* with my mom, that movie where Tom Cruise drives his autistic brother from Cincinnati to Los Angeles because his brother will not fly on an airplane. I had often been compared to Rain Man growing up, though my mother never liked it, as that character was much more disabled than I was. Anyways, when watching that movie I decided I would not want to do a cross country drive. I did not want to stay in ugly motels, I would get bored in the car, and I would not have all the things I was used to. However, as I got older and had a greater appreciation for different places, I changed my mind. Even before I stopped flying I decided I wanted to drive across the country. When I began hanging out in that California beach city, my goal was to go from Manhattan to Manhattan- Manhattan Beach, California to Manhattan, New York, and/or vice versa.

There were two things that stopped me from doing this trip. One was money, the other was my mother. Whenever I brought up driving all the way across the country, she said no. Part of it was the money, but I knew a big part of it was my Asperger's, and that to me was unjust. She said that even if I did not have Asperger's she would still be worried about me driving a car across the country. If I did not have my Asperger's, she probably would still be a bit worried as a mother, but much less so and probably would not have told me I could not do such a trip. Now that it came to West Virginia possibly being the only good place for me to move to and to my inability to fly, I would not let my parents telling me I could not drive across the country stop me from doing that. I would not let that stop me from going to the place where I could thrive.

Even though I was an adult, I could not simply take off on the trip without my parents' permission. It was their money and I would be using a lot of it. Ever since I was a child, I liked staying in upscale hotels on our trips. I always insisted in staying at the tallest hotel in the city we visited and on the highest floor they had, so that we could have a fabulous view, and with my father making a lot of money in the 1990s stock market boom, we could afford it. When I got to college and learned that college students stay in cheap motels or on the floors of people's houses, I would not do that. On a trip I took to Paris, I stayed on the 30th floor of a four star hotel on my own while my peers stayed at a cheap two star place. Eventually I toned down my insistence on the tallest hotel in the city and a view, but I still had to stay at the nice places like the Hiltons and Marriotts.

This was a major dilemma I faced. I did not get along with my parents, yet I was totally dependent on them financially since I did not have a job, and I had expensive tastes to top it off. However, this was not of my choosing. I was unable to get a job. Had society been less prejudiced of people with awkward social skills, speech patterns, and appearances that are beyond one's control, I could study something I was passionate about in college and get a good job in it that would let me do the things I like while getting paid, as I tried doing with my tourism major. Even if my job would not involve travel, or involve very little of it, I would still earn enough money to afford to travel on my own once in a while and stay in the nice hotels. When I graduated from college, I tried finding a job in the tourism industry or a related field, but no one would hire me. Neither would I be hired in Public Administration or Urban Planning jobs after getting my Master's. Besides the construction job that only lasted a year, the best I was offered were low paying jobs of arranging things at warehouses, flipping burgers, or bagging groceries, all jobs that I refused to take. While I do not think lowly of these workers, especially not in these pandemic times, for me taking these low skilled and low paying jobs would mean giving in to a system that puts down people like me.

One day I saw one of the girls from Honeycomb, my favorite store to hang out at in Manhattan Beach, sitting outside reading *Hillbilly Elegy* for school. I told her that I was glad her teacher gave her that book, as I wanted to move to West Virginia. She asked me why would I want to move to West Virginia. Indeed, many people were shocked that I wanted to move there. Even I was not so sure I wanted to. I didn't know how I would get used to rustic and poor West Virginia when I regularly hung out in the urbane and wealthy places in Southern California. But then again, many of the electrosensitives around Green Bank came from urban intellectual cultures like the one I came from, and many of the non-electrosensitive locals would also be fine people.

I was going to go in fall 2018, but we had too many expenses then so I could not convince my parents to agree at that time. Then came spring 2019, and I could not convince them either, having just had to get a new license at the DMV after losing my old one.

Being from Southern California, I needed to travel when the weather was right. I was never a fan of sweating, so I would not go to the humid eastern parts of the country in the summer. While I do not mind the cold as much as the heat, it does get extremely cold in much of the country and it is not too safe to drive in heavy snow. That left me with only spring and fall to do my drive. When I finally got my replacement license, it was heavy rains and allergies that set in much of the country. Once that was over, it got too close to summer. Now I had to wait until fall.

I was planning on going in September. My friend Colin went back to his hometown of Omaha one weekend every month to visit his mother and disabled brother, and I wanted to visit him when he was there. From Omaha, I would drive to New York to complete my cross country drive, then head to South Jersey to spend the Jewish High Holidays with my aunt, then go to that place in West Virginia without the cell phones and see if I wanted to move there, and then drive back home through the warmer south once the country would get colder. I was also planning on spending longer on my return segment than on the one heading out. When driving west, the sun would set in my eyes. I had a bad experience in Arizona in 2015 where I was nearly blinded after driving down a straight highway that went almost in the exact direction of the setting sun. Not wanting a repeat of that, I decided that when driving west I would not drive for two hours before sunset. Alternatively, I would take a road not going in the direction of the setting sun and only turn west after sunset. Even when driving back from Manhattan Beach I always waited until after sunset to drive west to Oxnard, which in the summer months meant sitting in my car reading long after the stores closed before I could drive back home.

When I checked the weather for the week Colin was to go, there was a heat wave along much of my route, so I would wait until his trip in October. That meant arriving in New Jersey after the holidays were over and when my aunt would be back at work teaching Hebrew school. As such, if I wanted to maximize my time with Colin and my aunt, I would need to see both of them on the weekends. Colin I could only see Friday night and Saturday morning, as his brother was having an episode and he wanted to spend all the time he could with him. That gave me another week until my aunt could see me, but with only a three or four day drive from Omaha to New Jersey, so I now would go to West Virginia between Omaha and New Jersey. A bit out of the way, but more worth my time and money.

Right as I was planning it all out, my parents called me one day saying they wanted me to cancel my trip. My dad looked up Green Bank and saw it was more than an hour away from any well sized town. I told him that I still wanted to go there and check it out. He retorted that we did not have money. I told him that the trip would be a few thousand dollars, but getting me a house in West Virginia instead of the one my parents had for me in Oxnard would be a savings of a few *hundred* thousand dollars. When he explained to me how much the taxes were on my house, I told him to sell it. Maybe I liked the finer things in life- nice hotels, nice houses, fine foods, but I wanted to have these things where they were affordable. Oxnard was a bit more affordable than Los Angeles, but not much more. In West Virginia, I could have a fabulous house for only 200 000 or just over. In Oxnard, the house in which I was cost three times as much. While my parents could afford that house for me, they could just barely afford it and I did not want to be in the situation where I had no money for other things such as travel or where my parents were struggling financially because of the expenses on my house. My father tried to explain that while a house there might be cheaper, I would also have a lot of maintenance costs. I told him that the savings in price would still outweigh that, and the taxes on a cheaper house would be much lower.

My parents told me that if I wanted to save money why would I not move back in with them. That I could not do. When I lived at home, I had very bad OCD that only relaxed once I moved out. I did not want to go back to those days.

My parents were not supportive of me moving to the middle of nowhere. I told them that I needed to move to that place in West Virginia. I needed to move there if I wanted to be away from cell phone radiation and somewhere more affordable. My mother said that I was talking about West Virginia the exact same way I was talking about Oregon before I moved there and that that did not work out. I told her this was not Oregon. This was a place where people did believe in the same things I did. It was not a place where people were the vaguely defined "liberal minded", but one where people actually avoided the exact same things I avoided and where the environment did not have in large quantities that thing that I avoided. Not only now were my parents not supportive of me moving there, they were not supportive of me checking it out, and that was not right.

And it was not only my parents. Some of my friends could also be ableist. Many people assumed I did not have a license at all and were actually surprised to learn I drive to places, even if they were only a few miles from my house. So you can imagine what the reaction of some of them was when I told them I would drive to New York.

Most of my friends did not tell me not to do it, but I did get into a big argument with Stasia over that matter. When I went to dinner with her a month before my trip, she told me not to drive at night. She had seen how I had a problem when a car with bright lights was heading my way. I explained to her that was only the case on narrow two lane roads but not on freeways where the lanes heading opposite directions are well separated from one another. I told her that I would simply stick to the freeways when driving at night. However, she would not have that. She told me not to drive at night at all. Without being able to drive the two hours before sunset on my return trip, it would mean that after the switch to daylight standard time I would need to end my day at 3 PM, and thus spend a lot of days and money on hotels. Now she told me to take a parent with me. When I told her that would not work, she said that maybe I should not go on that trip, and she even threatened to tell the DMV not to let me drive. Yes I could handle driving at night. I did that all the time driving back from Manhattan Beach on PCH. Even if bright lights did occasionally bother me, I handled it. Stasia still would not listen to me, rather being another person telling me I could not do this because of a disability. Now I yelled at her very loudly and then left. We did not talk for a month after that incident.

II.   Heading Out

My parents finally realized how important this trip was for me and agreed to let me go. October 15th would be my departure date, and it was on that day that I left my house in Oxnard and drove down PCH through Malibu as I always did. This time, however, I would not be returning after Manhattan Beach. I went to my parents' house to eat and to bid farewell to them. Then it was off to Manhattan Beach to officially inaugurate my trip. I parked right by the pier at 2 PM and met up with my friend Hailey, as we had planned on doing.

Hailey was someone who worked at the organic eatery in Downtown Manhattan Beach and gave me free frozen yogurt when they first opened. She was a very open minded young woman and one of the few people whom I considered a truly good friend. She indeed often seemed very concerned about me. Maybe it was in part due to the hard times she went through. She lost her father to a sudden heart attack when she was twelve. We walked along the pier, talking about my trip, neither of us believing I was actually about to do this. Hailey said that maybe I would not make it to New York, but that that still would be fine. I knew I would, however, but I told her I was worried I would get into an accident.

After walking along the pier, we went down to the beach where I tried filling up a bottle of water from the Pacific. It was a water bottle whose opening was rather narrow so it was difficult to fill it up. As such, Hailey, who is less afraid of water than I am, went farther into the ocean to fill it up for me, but also only managed to get it less than half full. I could not believe that in less than two weeks I would be doing this thing on the shore of another ocean that I would get to by car.

At 2:30 Hailey drove east on Manhattan Beach Boulevard to a meeting of hers while I also drove east on that road- to New York. I made a brief stop at Honeycomb telling the girls there that I was leaving for my trip. Then it was onto the 105 freeway. I planned my trip so that I would leave before rush hour traffic, but as soon as I passed the 405 interchange on the 105, even though it was still not yet 3:00, traffic became bumper to bumper. I got off the freeway to take the surface streets, as I always do in heavy traffic. Now I drove down Prairie Avenue, thinking that only in a few days I would be on the real prairie.

I am not sure how much faster surface streets are during traffic, but they are much less annoying than stop and go freeways and you are surrounded by fewer smog producing vehicles. Being someone who hates traffic even as I lived in one of the cities where it was the worst, I spent thirty years studying alternative roads in and around Los Angeles, as well as in other places, ever since I was old enough to understand maps and direction. I had been reading Thomas Guides, those guidebooks that used to be ubiquitous in Southern California before GPS, since my father first got me one when I was nine years old and have been studying them very well since then, memorizing a bunch of alternate roads both from the maps and from experience driving on them. When I tutored South Central teenagers in math as part of George W. Bush's No Child Left Behind program, I realized then that there is not too much traffic in South Central. Apparently this is because fewer people have cars there and not too many people from the better neighborhoods want to drive down the streets there.

When GPS first came into wide use, I was concerned that these systems would lead more people to the less crowded routes and that these routes would no longer not be jammed. Because many of the less crowded routes were on residential streets, I was worried that the residents would not like the increase in traffic and cause the cities to close turns onto their streets, thus forcing people to take the more crowded roads. Fortunately that did not happen to the extent I feared. I remember once a few years ago Waze started directing drivers in my parents' neighborhood onto residential streets. Eventually, however, the traffic volume on those small streets went down (or maybe people just stopped complaining). I think the solution was to tweak the algorithm as to not direct drivers onto those streets. I am much more in support of doing that than of restricting turns onto streets, as it reduces the traffic on the side streets while still allowing use by those who hate traffic enough to learn to read and analyze maps to figure out better roads to take without an algorithm doing it for them. As for me, I don't use GPS, as it gives off radiation. GPS that is built into the car and uses an external antenna I don't mind as much, as the radiation antenna is located outside the metallic cage in which one is seating. However, having thirty years' experience with paper maps, I still function well enough with them.

I was heading to the Angeles Crest Highway, as that was the closest place from where the freeway got jammed to an exit from the metropolitan area in the direction I was headed. To get there, I now had to pass through the neighborhoods just west of Downtown, which were crazy jammed and with no better alternatives. An hour and twenty minutes since I left Honeycomb, I had only driven twenty miles. But soon, barely three miles from the L.A. Civic Center, I made it onto the 2 freeway where traffic was all clear, because this freeway was headed to the mountains.

The 2 freeway soon became the notoriously windy Angeles Crest Highway. That road did have some traffic, mostly of people from the Pasadena area headed back home to Palmdale, but it was by no means jammed either. This is both because Palmdale and nearby Lancaster are not too populous and also because not too many people in L.A. want to take twisty mountain roads. But if you don't mind taking these roads and you absolutely abhor bumper to bumper traffic, they can be paradise. I stopped on a turnout in the road to clear my head of the electromagnetic fields from the cell towers I passed in the city and to have one final look back at the buildings of Downtown L.A. before leaving the region.

The Angeles Forest Highway, which I turned onto from Angeles Crest, seemed like it could be in Utah or many other places along my route, but I had to remind myself that I was still only fifty miles out of Manhattan Beach and less than one percent done with my trip. I turned onto Mount Emma Road right before Palmdale, along which I followed a trail of cars to make sure I was not reaching a dead end. By dusk I got to Victorville where I stopped at a Jack in the Box for a late lunch.

I got to Las Vegas at 9 PM, where I would spend my first night of this epic trip. I had been going to Vegas with my parents a lot as a child, and its themed hotels made it my favorite destination at one time. I like to tell about that time we first went there in 1992, right before my tenth birthday. In my younger years, we usually stayed in average three star hotels. Sometimes we would stay in more budget type motels, especially if a destination was expensive, but I never liked it when we did, such as on our trip to San Francisco that winter. Neither did I like staying at my grandmother's mosquito infested apartment in Israel that past summer, and when my mother and I visited the luxurious Hyatt she talked about staying there. Now on this trip, we originally stayed at the Excalibur, but when we got a bad room there we moved to the newly opened Mirage. Being Las Vegas, we could afford to stay at that luxury property, one with tropically scented corridors, lush landscaping both inside and out, and a grand swimming pool. After having stayed there once I never wanted to stay at a cheap motel again. In later years, as newer hotels were built on the Strip, the Venetian became a favorite of ours. Since I was traveling alone now, I had to stay in a bit more humble digs. I would not stay at the Motel 6 by the Tropicana, but rather at South Point, which was still a nice place. At only 79 dollars, it was the cheapest hotel I had for this trip.

My mother would have preferred me staying at the Motel 6. Maybe not in dangerous Las Vegas but everywhere else she would have preferred that. By the time I was in college, she tried to get me to stay at cheaper places, reminding me that we did not always stay somewhere nice. Here is my response to parents who don't want their children using their money on fine things. Don't introduce them to luxuries you cannot afford. Don't introduce your children to luxuries you cannot afford all the time, and don't introduce them to ones they might not be able to afford as adults unless you are prepared to pay for them. That is not to say don't take your children past the luxury homes of Beverly Hills, but don't give them the impression they will live there. If a place is cheap or you want to treat your children or yourself, you can take them to a more luxurious hotel once, but make sure they understand they will not be staying at that type of place all the time. After several years of staying at upscale properties, there was no going back for me.

Hailey used to live in Las Vegas, so she was quite familiar with that place and told me to be careful there at night. Luckily, I did not need to leave my hotel, as there were plenty of places to have dinner there. I went to the hamburger diner, which had good food but where there was still a bit too much exposure from cell phone radiation and secondhand smoke. The smoke is what I like least about casinos. Even if smoking is not allowed in the rooms I book or in the restaurants, you still get exposed to it when you need to walk through the casino to get everywhere, and it still gets into the restaurants.

In my room that night I was watching the Democratic presidential debates, where Elizabeth Warren was talking about her proposed wealth tax and not everyone was agreeing with her. I was getting quite a headache in my room. My room was quite close to the elevator and toward the back of the hotel, so I figured that I was right next to where the cell masts may have been placed only a couple floors above me. I asked to be moved farther away from the elevators, and I was now given a room at the way far end of a corridor, but still on the same floor. In the new room, I felt much better. My room was now facing eastward and I asked if I could be placed on the other side so that I would not have an intense sun coming in at 7 AM, but that was what they had available. I did enjoy the view from that 24th floor room, however, with it also being on the side of the building with the unobstructed views.

I was indeed awakened by the sun at 7 in the morning and decided to get up then. I did my traditional cruise down the Strip that I did whenever I was in Vegas. When I first went to Las Vegas in 1992, the Sands and the Dunes still dominated the Strip and the megaresorts were just beginning to go up. Each time I went there in the following years, another old hotel was gone to be replaced by a newer and much larger structure, structures that kept getting larger. Even though I liked the new hotels, I was also bitter about the city's neglect for its history when the old hotels got torn down or altered beyond recognition. However, over the past ten years, Las Vegas did not change much. You cannot add too much more to the Strip once it becomes full with 50 story buildings. Rather, most of the new construction is off the strip in non-central places that are as non-central as the original hotels on the Strip were when they were first built.

On this drive, I had a difficult time getting on the freeway once I passed downtown, as the signs are not always clearly marked and there are long waits at traffic lights, numerous trucks, and the strong *rising* sun of the desert was still low in my eyes. Usually the rising sun is not a problem for me, as I am not a morning person, but with the rising sun waking me up and deciding to leave my hotel right after, it was an issue this time. By the Strip the glare was made worse by the sun reflecting off the glass facades of the tall buildings. After I got on the freeway, I realized how tired I was so a bit outside of the city I got off and took a brief nap.

My original plan was to go from L.A. to Flagstaff and then from there to Moab, Utah, passing through places that I had never been to before such as Arches and Natural Bridges, and the following day I would drive to Denver. However, once I saw the hotel prices in Moab- $250 for a Best Western- I decided it was too expensive. I now thought of going to St. George on the first night and making it a two day drive to Denver. However, St. George to Denver would be a bit too far of a drive in one day. I also wanted to take the scenic two lane roads instead of the boring interstate for some of the way. That was what led me to the town of Escalante and the Canyon Country Lodge. I was thinking of driving there in one day from Oxnard, but I knew that even if I left Oxnard earlier I would not be able to get to Escalante before nightfall and the roads around there I did not want to drive at night.

I had first been to that part of southwestern Utah around St. George and Zion National Park in 2001 and my first impression was of the dramatic scenery and that that area was both very rural and very white. We had gone to a supermarket in the town of La Verkin and apparently its opening a month earlier was a big deal. Among the people there, virtually everyone, including the baggers, were white, which coming from L.A. was quite a culture shock. Now, however, that area was a huge suburban sprawl, stretching all the way from the Arizona border past where I got off on highway 9 to Zion and almost all the way to the park.

Once I got to Zion National Park, I had to pay a 35 dollar admission fee even if I was just driving through. I decided I would just get the 80 dollar annual pass for all the parks, especially as I was going to visit more parks on this trip. The road through Zion was indeed very scenic, with the red rock formations, the plants growing through them, and that mile long tunnel carved though the rocks. I soon was on the highway headed to Bryce Canyon. I at first was not planning on going there, as I had already been there on that trip in 2001, and I wanted to get to my hotel early. However, once I got to the junction for Bryce, I decided that I did not want to pass right by without going there, and it had been eighteen years since I was last there. Plus, I had my annual pass so I did not need to worry about the fees. I went into the park and the first overlook very quickly, as I still wanted to get to my hotel early and catch up on my sleep. I parked on the side of the road, walked down the short trail, and when I got to the edge of the cliff looked at the dramatic rock formations around me. I remembered this place very well from eighteen years earlier, as well as the fight I had with my parents that day. After that one overlook, I was ready to go back to the main highway and to my hotel.

The highway went through Grand Staircase- Escalante, the National Monument established by Bill Clinton in 1996 and that Trump recently shrank in size by nearly half. Driving through the various unspoiled landscapes on highway 12, I was wondering if that was still part of the monument (most of that stretch is not) and very much hoping it does not get taken up by developers just like the stretch of road before Zion had been taken up in recent years.

I arrived at my hotel at 4:30, happy to be there at an early time. It was a two story hotel and I asked for a room on the second floor when I was given one on the first. The woman at the desk told me that that was the only room they had. I told her that I was surprised the hotel would be full on a weekday in October. She told me that they had been booked for the past three weeks. I told her that maybe it was because of global warming. Indeed it was unseasonably hot in the 70s that day.

I then tried to take a nap in my room but could not fall asleep. The older woman working at the front desk was nice and helpful, and she told me she liked living in that town of only 800 people. The younger people working there, however, did not really want to interact with anyone beside their peers and their phones. I have noticed that younger people, likely due to everything one hears about in the media, have become distrustful of older generations. I used the computer in the lobby to send some e-mails and look up some things. The computer used wi-fi, but there was an Ethernet connection in the wall and I was able to connect my cable to it, turn off the wi-fi, and connect to the Internet in a wired manner. I also tried using the phone in my room to call my parents, as they wanted me to call them every night once I got to my hotel, but the phone did not work. I asked the woman at the reception about it and she told me that I only the manager could fix that and he would not be in until 10 PM or later. I did not want to wait that long for him, wanting to go to bed early, so I just e-mailed my parents saying that I had arrived.

The following morning, I met another employee of the hotel and Escalante local who was nice. She asked me if I wanted to sit with her for breakfast and I said yes. We talked until her friend Katie who was on her phone walked by. I got up, but came back a minute later once Katie was no longer on her phone. Then when she got back on her phone, I got back up again. When I walked back over once Katie was no longer on her phone, the first woman asked if I really did not want to sit with them. I told her that I am sensitive to cell phones, at which time Katie put hers away. Katie was also working at that hotel and told me she was from a nearby city along the Interstate. I told her that I was actually thinking of staying at that town but I saw they did not have anything there better than a Quality Inn, as was the case with most non-touristy small towns along those routes. Even the hotel where I was staying in was the only first class hotel in town and before it was built two years prior there were none there. I talked quite at length with these two workers, both about my trip and places I was thinking of moving to. I was beginning to wonder whether that town might be a good place for me. It was way closer than West Virginia.

I had a very scenic drive down the rest of highway 12 the following day, with the road at once going through a narrow red rock canyon and then on top of a dramatic mountain ridge. At one point I saw some animals on the road, and as I got closer I could not believe what it was- cowboys. They were on horses parading cattle down the highway, and I was surprised people still do that in this day and age. The road soon made a steep descent into the town of Torrey, where I made a right turn onto highway 24 to go to my first new national park- Capitol Reef. I explored that park briefly, with its dramatic red rocks and the preserved buildings of the abandoned community of Fruita. I followed the 24 for another hour and a half down the canyon of the park to where it gradually opened to reveal a deserty landscape which remained with me until and past the point I got to I-70.

When I already was on my way I had realized that I did not have one of my bags with me. I thought maybe it was in the trunk. However, when I took a brief nap at a freeway exit, I decided to check my trunk and my bag was not there. I had several important things in that bag- including the cable I used to connect to the Internet wiredly. It was too late to go back to the hotel to pick it up, as it was at least a four hour drive by now. I told myself that once I would get to Denver I would call the hotel in Escalante and ask them to mail the bag to me.

I stopped for lunch in Grand Junction, Colorado. While there, I realized the people over there were very friendly, as I had realized of other parts of the state on previous trips, and was now thinking of adding Grand Junction to my list of possible places to move to. Past Grand Junction, the road entered the Rockies, slowly climbing through the various canyons and valleys of the Colorado River before hitting what is likely the most dramatic stretch of Interstate in the United States. That is the stretch through Glenwood Canyon. Due to the narrowness of the canyon and also due to environmental concerns, it took nearly two decades to plan and construct and was the last section of a major Interstate to be built in the United States. As recently as 1992, this fifteen mile stretch was still a two lane highway. The architecture of this roadway was truly interesting, with the graceful curves of the upper roadway built on top of a concrete wall that resembled the architecture of some 1980s malls, and with the backdrop of the sheer walls of the canyon. Unfortunately, while that highway was supposed to improve traffic flow, it did not, at least not at the time I was on the road. Traffic narrowed to only one lane on my side due to construction and for about five miles I was stuck only going ten miles an hour behind large gas spewing trucks

When I was stuck in traffic in the canyon, I had to go to the restroom. I do not pull off at highway rest areas to do that, as I need a clean, quiet, and odor free restroom, and these are not found everywhere. I decided I would stop in Vail, as that was right along the highway and an iconic place. I got off the freeway in downtown Vail, after having sat in my car for more than two hours that seemed forever. I went to the main parking lot of the "Village" and was appalled at the rates. The first ten minutes were free, but 11 to 30 minutes was 12 dollars, 31 to 60 minutes was 22 dollars, and another hour was another ten dollars. Even Beverly Hills did not charge this much for parking. Nevertheless, I did not want to drive all around the city looking for parking when I really had to go to the restroom and did not want to arrive in Denver too late. I went to the restroom in the upscale hotel above the parking structure, then briefly walked around the Village, where I have to say that the people seemed polite but not the most friendly. I spent a total of twenty minutes there, paying twelve dollars for parking. Once I got back to my car, I had past exactly a thousand miles since I left Manhattan Beach.

I wanted to do as much driving before 6 PM, when they would start closing down lanes of the freeway for road work. I did not quite make it before 6, but fortunately I only had a lane closure in one small part. I was there on October 17th at 6:04 PM, 5:04 PM Pacific time and exactly thirty years to the minute since the San Francisco earthquake of 1989. I still remember from when I was seven years old watching the news of that quake as it happened. To commemorate the anniversary, I shook my steering wheel to create an earthquake sensation. Five minutes later, coincidentally enough, I was driving through the town of Frisco.

Past Frisco, I climbed past 11000 feet to the Eisenhower Tunnels that would take me under the Continental Divide. I was quite low on gas at this point, but it was also almost all downhill from there to Denver so I would still have enough gas to make it there. I got to my hotel at 7:30, getting off at one exit to look at my map to see where my hotel was. Denver was where my college friend Ryan lived. I met up with him there in 2016 when I was thinking of moving to the Denver area, and I had planned to meet up with him again this time. I called him as soon as I got to my hotel and asked him to meet me at the same Moroccan restaurant in Aurora we went to the previous time.

I filled up my tank before heading out to meet Ryan. At the restaurant, there were quite a few people on their cell phones, including a kid of about eleven who was the nephew of the owners who did some table cleaning there and would sometimes walk by our table with his phone. We had to ask him to stop doing that. Afterward, it was back to my hotel. I was now exhausted and ready to go to bed. Nevertheless, I called the hotel in Escalante and they told me they had my bag. They told me to call Katie the following morning and that she could mail it to me. Then I called my parents. My father answered, but my mother was not at home, having gone to stay with my uncle after his wife was taken to the hospital and he did not want to be alone, having had a stroke a couple months prior. I would try calling my mother back the following morning, as I was too tired now.

I went to sleep at 11, not falling asleep immediately, and got up the following morning at 7. I was still too tired then, so I tried going back to sleep and slept for another hour, after which I felt wide awake. I called Katie and she told me she could send my bag through the Postal Service. I originally wanted FedEx to do it, but she assured me the Postal Service was better, especially from small towns that FedEx did not drive to every day. She talked to her husband who worked for the Postal Service and he said they could have it delivered within a week. I gave her the address of my aunt in New Jersey, which was where I would be then, and asked her to send it there. Then I called my mother at my uncle's place. My mother had gone to yoga. Not wanting to wait until she was done and there not being a landline phone at Colin's house where I would be staying that night, I would not talk to my mother until the night after.

The freeway started off fine, but as soon as I got to Downtown Denver the bottlenecks began. I got off and took the surface streets right past City Hall and the State House. I passed through various neighborhoods that reminded me of Portland before getting to I-76 leading toward Omaha and that I hoped would not be jammed. It indeed was not jammed, and I drove on that road past the industrial areas and trailer parks on the city's outskirts. The city had a good amount of sprawl and more than twenty miles from downtown there were some new developments being built. However, soon the sprawl ended and now looking around me there was a sea of prairie.

I continued on the Interstate for some distance, but when I got to the junction of U.S. 6 eighty miles from Downtown Denver, I decided to get off and take the old U.S. highway instead. That road proved so much more interesting than the freeway. It went right through the farm fields instead of in the hills above it. It followed the natural contours of the land rather than slicing through it. It had only a few cars here and there as opposed to the multitude of gas spewing trucks on the Interstate, and also fewer cell towers right by the road. And the speed limit in most stretches was 65, only ten miles per hour less than the freeway and only slowing down through the occasional town. I would avoid the "genetically modified landscapes" of the Interstates as much as feasible.

Soon U.S. 6 turned away from the freeway and now I took U.S. 138, which was the new route paralleling I-76. I kept seeing signs at junctions saying to take that road to the freeway, but averaging more than sixty miles an hour on the old highway I ignored them. Soon I passed into Nebraska. I crossed under I-80, the interstate going to Omaha, but did not enter. I continued on to the next town, where I got out of my car after driving three hours straight from Denver. It was cloudy and a strong wind was blowing, but not too cold- the temperature was in the 60s. As I was walking around the central part of this small town, I was thinking to myself that I finally reached Middle America and the Plains, and that this is what an old small town there looks like.

III. Middle America

If I was not going to take the Interstate, the main road leading to Omaha now would be U.S. 30- the old Lincoln Highway. I made a right turn in that town past the railroad tracks, thinking that was U.S. 30. It was not- it was the road leading to the freeway. I turned back around, this time having to wait for a train to cross, to take that road back through town and two miles in the other direction to join U.S. 30. The 30 proved to be like the other U.S. highways, passing through farmland with a 65 miles per hour speed limit that only slowed down once a small town would be hit every ten miles. Soon I got to North Platte, the first big town on the road. I stopped there for lunch at a Taco Time. After lunch, I looked at my atlas to see how far I was from Omaha. I was still 276 miles away. It was 4:30 now, and I told Colin I would be at Omaha at around 8:00. If I wanted to get there not much later than 8:00, I would need to get back on the boring Interstate.

I wanted to continue a bit farther down the old highway with its towns and grain silos. I stayed there for another twenty miles until the town of Gothenburg, whose name I found interesting because it was that of a city in Sweden, at which point I was ready to get back on the Interstate. I now took the freeway through the desolate landscape. I thought of getting off at some places while there was still daylight and going back to the old road, but I also did not want to arrive at Nick's too late and for both of us to be too tired to do much. But then again, the Interstate did have some scenic places where it crossed and had rest stops along the Platte River, another historic highway along which Indian and later emigrant trails ran, which were the forerunners of the modern highways we have today. Soon I approached sunset. While driving opposite the direction of the setting sun is usually not a problem, it is once you have large trucks and road signs with reflective surfaces, as was the case on the Interstate. While not as bad as driving into the setting sun, it was still a bit uncomfortable for about half an hour.

I made it to Colin's house right before 8:30. We went with his mother to a Greek restaurant where a very un-Greek Omaha steak was on the menu. I noticed that cell phone use at restaurants there was not only a little less than in California, but a lot less. I had talked with Colin several times about moving to Omaha once I realized many of the liberal places I wanted can also be socially isolating. He told me that cell phone use there would be lower, but I did not expect it to be that low. This was the least amount of cell phone use I had seen in a big city since the smartphone revolution, with the possible exception of Portland. Colin also told me there would not be too many dogs there. People still had dogs for hunting and to guard their properties, but they would not be found nearly as much in the stores or on the streets. People would be friendly and caring there, but he also warned me that it was a conservative place. He told me that some people might be reactionary to my unorthodox ways and not afraid to confront me over them. I became familiar with the Midwestern type in high school where a couple of my teachers were from that region. They were all people committed to helping me, but they also could be quite strict about me doing things a certain way. The Midwest also had the harsh weather- the freezing cold winters, the hot and humid summers, and not to mention the occasional storms and tornadoes. West Virginia also had unpleasant weather, but the area around Green Bank was actually quite mild for the east coast, with summers not too hot and humid and winters cold but not as cold as the Upper Midwest.

That evening, when talking more about the people of Omaha, Colin told me there were plenty of liberals there even if the place was conservative leaning, and that Omaha was more liberal than the rest of the state. We saw one of the friendly Omahans for ourselves when we got into a long conversation with the checkout lady at a Walgreen's who told us that she had lived in Baltimore and Florida but recently moved to Omaha and liked it better. The only thing that kept me from moving there now was the weather.

One good thing about Omaha was that I did not need to worry about finding a hotel. Colin had two houses available for me- the one where he was staying with his mother and the one where the mother used to live and which was now empty and in the process of being sold. I stayed at the empty house, which still had the utilities turned on as well as furniture and beds. The following morning, I went to Colin's to go with him to pick up his brother from the foster family with whom he was living in a suburb. We then went to a landmark seafood eatery in town for lunch. It was nice to finally meet Colin's brother after having heard a lot about him for the past sixteen years. His skull had an excess amount of fluid, which caused him to have severe balance issues and considerable intellectual impairment. Yet, Colin, his mother, and his foster family did take very good care of him.

After lunch and briefly hanging out at the house of Colin's mother, he had to have his alone time with his brother. That was when I left to drive across Iowa to the border with Illinois, where I would be spending the night. I was thinking of driving to Wisconsin, as it had very liberal places that would be have west coast liberalism combined with the friendliness and values of the Midwest, but that would be too far out of the way and even colder than Omaha, so I skipped it. I now headed to Downtown Omaha to check it out. It was one of the least annoying big city downtowns I had seen yet, with the traffic being very smooth flowing through the high rise district. South of there was the section with the old three to four story brick buildings, which was very lively with its boutiques and restaurants and with the brick roadways and carriage rides giving the place an old fashioned feel.

Then it was across the Missouri River into Iowa. I got off of the I-480 bridge as soon as I crossed and drove through the central part of Council Bluffs. I followed a sign for the Lincoln Highway right through the historic downtown, which was filled with local businesses and some boutiques, but nothing as fancy as those in coastal California towns. I followed the Lincoln Highway signs outside of downtown, and soon found myself on a windy road through Iowa's hill country. Soon I noticed where the sun was shining and realized I was heading north when I should have been going east. I stopped on the side of the road to check my map, and decided to stay on that road until it would merge a bit farther down with U.S. 30. Then I would take scenic highway 44 east, which would lead me straight into Des Moines and the path of I-80.

Highway 44 did prove to be very scenic, even though it was Iowa. It was a mostly straight road that in its first section went straight up and down hills in a landscape covered with cornfields and grain silos. The road passed among farmhouses with farmers riding their John Deeres. Eventually the landscape flattened, but now there was the occasional town- towns with main streets and, in the case of the larger ones, plazas. They had neat whitewashed houses- some with Halloween decorations. In one town I passed right by their annual fall/ Halloween pageant. By 5:15, the housing density increased as I was passing through the outskirts of Des Moines.

I-80 circumvented the central part of Des Moines and getting on that route now would have been a more direct route. However, I did not want to miss seeing Des Moines so I looped a bit south to take I-235 into the city. I got off from that freeway on 31st street and took the surface streets through the historic neighborhoods into downtown. I found the metropolitan center of Iowa to be a very livable city, just like Omaha. It had a good central core with restaurants and pedestrian friendly streets that were alive that Saturday evening. The only issue I had was with the setting sun right behind me that reflected off the tall buildings and the covered pedestrian overpasses.

Des Moines has just over 200 000 people, the same population as Oxnard. Yet Des Moines felt much more like a city than where I lived. Des Moines has a downtown filled with tall buildings, yet Oxnard has only two significantly tall buildings, both of which are in a business park rather than in downtown. Many California and Sunbelt cities of that size lack tall buildings. This is both because these cities only became large ones in recent decades, as opposed to cities in the rest of the country that have been large for much longer, and also because of a general resistance to tall buildings in those places. To people in California, adding tall buildings to a formerly small town means that the place is growing too big. But guess what, once a city reaches 200 000 it is no longer a small town. It is now a medium sized city. If a center with tall buildings is not built up, there is much less of a community feel and sprawl is encouraged. Des Moines, despite having the worse weather, did seem much more lively than Oxnard or similarly sized Santa Clarita.

Des Moines is also mentioned in what might be the greatest opening line from a travel narrative. "I come from Des Moines. Somebody had to." This is from Bill Bryson's *The Lost Continent,* another book about a transcontinental drive. I am a huge fan of travel narratives, having read many of them, both classics that I printed off the Internet if they were public domain, and more contemporary accounts. I have never been much of a fan of fiction, save for a few classics and a few authors I like. These works are often too depressing and are never realistic, no matter how realistic they are presented as being. And if it is a work of fiction that I like, I would rather see the movie. Nonfiction, however, is real. It is about real people, real life, and, when it comes to travel books, real adventures.

Travel narratives are not for everyone, though. A few years back, a teacher in Manhattan Beach assigned her eighth grade class John Steinbeck's *Travels With Charley* for their summer reading. Though that is one of the great classics of the genre, supposedly none of her students liked it and she never assigned that book again.

I got back on the freeway after Des Moines. My hotel was in the Quad Cities, that region of Davenport and Bettendorf, Iowa, and, on the other side of the Mississippi River, Rock Island and Moline, Illinois. My hotel was in East Moline. I was thinking of getting off the freeway in Davenport to see that place, but I decided not to as it was getting late. I continued onto the bridge over the wide Mississippi, and was quite excited to have gotten that far by car. My hotel was a bit difficult to find, as River Road was closed due to a flood risk. Rather, I had to take the roads that went deeper into the city. While Davenport seemed nice from the pictures I saw, Moline was quite ghetto. While its rows of wooden whitewashed houses might have made for a good place to live at one time, it was now clearly a run down area.

I soon found my hotel. It was a newly built nine story building right along the Mississippi. When I checked in, they could not find my reservation, so I had to make a new one. Luckily this place was not full and I was able to get a room with a river view. I did not want to drive around at 9:30 looking for a place to have dinner, so I had it at the hotel's restaurant. When I was in my room, I called my parents and I was finally able to reach my mom after five days on the road. She could not believe that I had gotten to the Mississippi either. She asked me if I was not tired from all of these driving. No, I told her. I still enjoyed the driving and all the places I was seeing. Maybe I was getting a bit tired, but I still had my hotels at night where I was getting a good sleep. And the river view I had from this hotel was spectacular.

The following morning, it was quite cold. Up until now I had very good weather with highs in the 70s. That morning, however, it was in the low 50s, which made it a bit uncomfortable to pack my car. For the first leg of my trip, I again took the old highways. Now it was U.S. 150, which paralleled I-74, the Interstate going all the way to Cincinnati, my next night's destination. I stayed on U.S. 150 for about an hour, passing through rolling hills of cornfields. Unlike Nebraska, the speed limit on the old highways was now only 55 and the towns were closer together, so if I did not want to get to Cincinnati too late I had to get back on the freeway.

I stayed on the freeway until I got to Peoria, where I wanted to see the "Will it play in Peoria" city and got back onto the 150. The 150 went through a couple neighborhoods before going on a scenic bridge over the Illinois River when I looked behind me to see the buildings of Downtown Peoria and realized the highway bypassed them. I took the roads along the river back to Downtown Peoria, hoping to find a good place to have lunch there. That did not turn out to be a good quality downtown. While it had some nice old tall buildings, the place was quite abandoned, albeit with some revitalization efforts. There was no place to eat there, so I went back across the river to a new shopping center. I checked out a sandwich place as well as a Southwestern one, but before I could look at the menu, crowds of diners were standing in my way. I decided to go to the next town over.

Driving through South Peoria, I hit Springfield Road, and turned onto it thinking Springfield would be my next city. However, seeing the position of the sun and that I was heading south instead of southeast, I checked my map at the next traffic light and realized Springfield was not in the direction I was planning to head. I made a left turn and soon was back on U.S. 150 paralleling I-74, the latter of which I got on at the next onramp. Soon, however, there was some construction and the freeway narrowed to only one lane which the traffic only going 50, along with a multitude of trucks on the road. This was about the same speed as the old highways, if not slower, so I got off the freeway at the next offramp and took the much more beautiful and less crowded 150 instead. The next sizable city was Normal, and U.S. 150 bypassed it through an industrial park west of town. I immediately turned to the central part of town, not wanting to miss a city with such an interesting name. Normal to me is only the city with the second most unusual name in Illinois. The one with the most unusual name is another place I would later drive through.

In the central part of Normal, I hit another historic highway- Route 66. Route 66 is the quintessential highway for American road trippers who do not like the doldrums of the Interstate. For me, it was also another thing. It was the road home. It was the route I took back home on more than one trip through Arizona and New Mexico. It was also a road of home. Its last leg was Santa Monica Boulevard, a major street only a couple miles from where I grew up and along which I had ridden many times to and from school, my uncle's place, the parks, the malls, and other places, and along which were Persian restaurants and stores I regularly frequented with my family long before I even knew of Route 66 or its significance. Now I was in Illinois, near the other end of that road, on a road that goes home. And heading west on it (technically south, but west as far as the general route of the highway), I felt like I was going home.

In Bloomington, the town directly adjacent to Normal, U.S. 150 turned east from the 66 and I turned with it. However, I immediately realized that I was only a block north of downtown and the 66 would lead straight through it, so I turned back around to take that route. I stopped for lunch in downtown Bloomington, another fairly run down downtown with some attempts at revitalization. Most of the places were closed there, as it was Sunday, but I did find one Chicago style Greek deli open there (I was only 150 miles from the Windy City). I got an Italian beef sandwich. I personally think that should be renamed Chicago Beef of Southern European Immigrants, or better yet, Chicago Lunch Counter Beef, as that dish of thinly sliced beef it not found on any authentic Italian menus that I know of.

Main Street soon got to I-74 and I entered the freeway. I got off right before I reached Mahomet. That is the Illinois town whose name I find most unusual. If you are familiar with old Anglicizations of foreign names, you might know that Mahomet is an obsolete form of Muhammad. While driving though that town, I was wondering if most of its 8400 residents know that. An interesting coincidence occurred while I was driving through the center of town and, on the oldies station I was listening to, Moonshadows by Cat Stevens, who later became a follower of Muhammad, came on.

Five miles past Mahomet is Champaign, the Illinois city with the third most interesting name- interesting because it is like the name of a fancy wine but spelled differently, and also because it is one letter away from campaign, which I used to think was the city's pronunciation. Champaign is home to the University of Illinois, and I headed through the central part of the city before going to the college. I used to be a huge fan of Microsoft Flight Simulator. When I was a child and the scenery consisted of nothing but green ground in most places in the game, the University of Illinois was highly detained, showing the school's football field and the tall buildings of Champaign. In Flight Simulator 5, I remember there was a building near the football field with an Easter egg. There was a mysterious opening that you could go through and inside was a picture of the creators of Flight Simulator.

Champaign and the University of Illinois looked very different in real life than in the primitive early 90s versions of the computer game. Rather, with the design of the city, the situation of the university east of the city, and the university's brick buildings with broadleaf trees shedding their leaves reminded me of one particular city in which I was at one time- Eugene. I walked around the campus a little, going into one of the historic buildings and using the restroom there. Then I walked into one elegant looking building. It turned out to be the student union and was covered in rich wood panelings- indeed very fancy for a student union. But it was also full of another thing- wireless radiation. I immediately walked out of that building. I was thinking to myself how can college students handle being surrounded by all the multitudes of people on their wireless devices irradiating them. Aren't there many college students who are electrosensitive. Maybe there are not many who realize they are, but there are many who drop out of college because they start getting headaches and the like.

On the other side of the university was the town of Urbana, with its historic center of whitewashed houses among green lawns. Urbana, with its Latin urban name, is the Illinois city with the fourth most interesting name. It is interesting to note that Urbana means a city place while Champaign means a place of fields- i.e. the country. However, Champaign is now the much bigger city.

In the next town over from the city place, I turned to get back on the freeway. Soon, however, there was again construction and the freeway again narrowed to one lane. As soon as I got to an exit, I got off and got back to the 150 and its towns. I stayed there for about ten miles until the old highway crossed the freeway and I got back on it. I stayed on the freeway for maybe seven miles this time before seeing a sign for another upcoming lane closure. I got off at the next exit, before the closure began. While going through the previous city, I saw an exit to the 150 where it appeared to cross the freeway again, so I assumed that the 150 was now south of the freeway, but I was not sure. Once I got off, I turned south, pulled over to look at my atlas, and saw that the 150 had now taken a different course away from the freeway and the new road paralleling the freeway was U.S. 136, running to the north. I turned around to get to the 136 and followed it east straight into Indiana. Once I was over the border, I considered getting back on the freeway, but it was now right before sunset and I knew there would be the glare from the trucks. Also, I did not know if the construction had ended. While driving down these two lane highways that were not much slower than the Interstates even when the Interstates did not have construction, I was wondering why did we have to spend billions of dollars on the Interstates. But then again, I saw the old highways with almost none of the traffic using them. Had the Interstates not been built and the high volume of traffic we have now had to use the old two lane highways, the traffic on them could be slower than on an L.A. freeway at rush hour.

I had been on U.S. 136 for at least twenty miles when it crossed back under the freeway. I was not sure about lane closures, but I saw that there were still construction cones in the freeway. I was wondering if the construction was really covering that long of a stretch. These freeway repairs do not only cover long stretches, but also long time periods. On a popular Youtube video of a time lapsed cross country drive that was filmed on the same stretch of I-74 and made in 2017- two years before I made my trip- this construction was also going on. The only difference was that the stretches of freeway not under construction then where the one under construction when I made my trip.

I got back to the freeway once the sun had gone down and I reached U.S. 41, which made me think of the highway's reference in the Allman Brothers' song "Ramblin' Man". When I got on the freeway, there were still construction cones, but apparently this was right where the construction ended. The highway opened back up to both lanes. I stayed on the freeway until I got to Indianapolis, where I got off at the western end of the city to take 10th Street to Downtown. I told myself once in the 2000s that when I would make it to Indianapolis I would like to both do a Cherokee dance and eat Indian food, in reference to the two kinds of Indians. The first thing is no longer politically acceptable. However, I did get Indian food in Indianapolis. I stopped at a shopping plaza off of Tenth at the edge of downtown and found an Indian restaurant there. The food was not authentic at all and I did not even see any Indians working there- it was all blacks and one white person. They had a few types of meats where you selected the curry and the curry was poured straight over the meat- not the way to cook Indian food, you need to cook it with the curry. Nevertheless, the restaurant was an experience.

I drove down Tenth to Meridian, which is the city's main street, and it was indeed very lively over there. The city had some grand landmarks that were brightly lit, including the large Soldiers' Memorial and the column in the city's central plaza. The city was full of restaurants and carriage rides with strings of colored lights on them. I drove straight through the downtown and then got back on the freeway, this time to Cincinnati.

Over the course of one day, I started at the border of Illinois and drove straight across the state. Then I entered Indiana and drove straight across it also. Now I had made it to Ohio. I still had another thirty miles to go to my hotel, which was in the Cincinnati suburb of Blue Ash. My hotel was a bit hard to find. I drove around the streets of the business parks of Blue Ash for about ten minutes until I found the well hidden Embassy Suites. That was the longest day on the trip for me so far, not having reached my hotel until after 10:30. I hoped that I would get to my hotel sooner the next day, and the next day I would be in the Quiet Zone of West Virginia!

I got up the following morning, driving down the streets of Cincinnati through downtown. I had heard some good things about Cincinnati, including how Winston Churchill once described it as the most beautiful inland city in the United States. It did indeed have a beautiful riverfront along the Ohio River with its well landscaped park. I had long been fascinated by the 1867 Roebling Bridge, with it being a precursor to the Brooklyn Bridge- it was designed in the same style and by the same architect- and having been the longest suspension bridge in the world when first built. I drove on the bridge now into Kentucky, the eleventh state on this trip so far and the fourth that I had never been to before. I would have more of Kentucky to explore on my drive back, now it was back over to the Ohio side and to a scenic drive down the Ohio River.

I had read accounts of people sailing down the Ohio- both Charles Dickens in the pioneer days of the Ohio Valley and someone who did it in the 1990s when he sailed all the way across the United States by boat using minimal portaging- so it was quite exciting to be driving along the river now. It was a scenic corridor lined with rolling hills on either side of the river, but the view was sometimes marred by a power plant. I stopped for lunch at the restaurant of a motel with the unlikely name of the Beverly Hills Inn.

After lunch, I got to a place where the sign said "Road closed 1.4 miles ahead"- At least that was what it appeared to say- and pointed to a detour. I was sad to leave the course of the river behind and get onto a road with more trucks that would add more than ten miles to my drive. I hoped that at the next highway I could go back to the river road, and sure enough there was a detour sign at the next highway point back to that road. I turned onto that highway, but as soon as I got to the river road there was a road closed 7 miles ahead sign. I thought it might be a mistake, so I turned onto that road and sure enough after seven miles the road was closed. I thought of trying to ask the construction workers if they could let me through, but I just turned around, having wasted more than half an hour on that detour. Apparently, the first sign had said "road closed 14 miles ahead", but with the way the 1 and the 4 were spaced it looked like there was a decimal between them.

I soon was back by the river, but now I just wanted to take the fastest roads to Green Bank because that place was far from the freeway and I wanted to minimize driving down two lane roads at night. I took the freeway straight through the cities of Huntington and Charleston, West Virginia, not getting off in them. I only got off once I passed Charleston where the freeway no longer took a direct route and U.S. 60 was not my direct route. I took that road over the mountains and once I got down into the mountain valleys I-64 rejoined the 60 and I got on it briefly. I exited in Lewisburg, which was the closest sizable town to Green Bank and still more than an hour away. There were signs from the freeway saying that Lewisburg was voted the coolest small town in the United States by a certain magazine, and another one pointing to its historic center. At the freeway exit, I turned south away from Green Bank to get to that center. It was nighttime already, so I did not need to worry about doing more night driving. However, there was another concern. I did not want to get to my hotel too late. That was a small, non corporate place so there would not be 24 hour service and I did not want to get locked out because I arrived late. It was now 7:45 PM. My plan was to get to my hotel in a timely manner and then find a place in town that would be open late or to have some hot food at the hotel if they had any.

IV. West Virginia

I drove down the at times windy U.S. 219 to get to my hotel. I did not have too many problems with blinding lights, as that road was largely empty. I passed through the 1000 resident town of Marlinton, the nearest sizable town to Green Bank. My hotel would be located between Marlinton and Green Bank. The closer I got to Green Bank, the less radio stations could be heard. When I was by my hotel, only three FM stations were audible, all of which were low power ones playing the same thing. The roads were dark, with a dead dear apparently struck by another car lying in the middle of the road at one place. Then I saw a sign for my hotel and some lights in the distance. After overshooting the turn, I turned back around to get onto the dirt road leading to my hotel. I was thinking of the opening scene to the 80s miniseries The Thorn Birds where Richard Chamberlain drives down a dirt road to a remote ranch in Australia to what will be his new assignment for years and where he falls in love. I was singing the theme music from that series to myself and thinking to myself if that would indeed be the new place where I would live.

It was now just past 9 PM. I walked into the brightly lit hotel looking for the office. I soon found the office and the person sitting at the desk and told him I was checking in. He seemed like a nice person, and he told me that he was a transplant from Utah. He was not electrosensitive, but he moved there because he liked the area. I immediately asked him if there were any restaurants nearby that were still open and he told me that not at that time and that all of them close early. He offered me some snacks for dinner, but that would not suffice. Just like I had a rule about not letting a dog lick me, I had one about having a warm dinner that was hearty. I asked him if anything in Marlinton would still be open, and he told me that he believed some places would be open there till 10, but he asked me if I was sure I wanted to drive the twenty miles there. I had already driven 2800 miles across the country, so twenty miles to get there was not a big deal. He wanted to check me in and give me a whole tour of the hotel, but I asked him if he could wait for me to get back from Marlinton so that I would be sure the restaurants were still serving once I got there. He told me that by the time I would get back he would be asleep, so I let him check me in. Then he wanted to give me a tour of the property. I told him no, as I wanted to get to Marlinton on time. Again, he offered me to just have some snacks or to warm up some leftover soup for me, but I told him no- that I really needed to have a dinner. He let me go without having a tour, and then I drove as fast as I could to Marlinton.

I arrived in town right after 9:30, but there was a problem. All the restaurants closed no later than 9. Even the Dairy Queen closed at 9. I asked a gas station attendant if he knew of any restaurants in town that were open late, and he told me that there were none. So now if I did not want to be stuck with cold snacks, my only choice was to drive back to Lewisburg.

I was no stranger to going out of my way to get the type of food and drinks that I will not do without. One time when I was in St. Petersburg, Russia and my tour group was taken to a restaurant with no juice or soft drinks on the menu, I went out of the restaurant looking for them. I will not drink water, as it tastes bland, and neither will I drink alcohol. There were plenty of stalls on the street selling soft drinks, but they only took Russian money, and not the Euros or credit cards I had on me. I walked back to the Hermitage museum we were at right before the restaurant, stood in a long Soviet style line for their coffeeshop, and when I got to the end saw a sign that even there they did not take non Russian money. I had to exchange my Euros in the gift shop and then I was able to get a drink. By the time I got back to the restaurant, more than an hour had passed, my parents were terribly worried, and I had to take my food on the bus right as our group was ready to board.

On this drive to Lewisburg, I hoped I would find a place there that was still open. If not, my plan was to drive two hours to Charlottesville, where I was sure there would be places open 24 hours (it's a college town), get a hotel as I would be too tired to drive back to Green Bank, and then try to negotiate with the hotel in Green Bank to not charge me for the first night. As soon as I crossed the freeway into Lewisburg, I went to the first restaurant- Ruby Tuesday. They were closed- they closed at 10. The restaurant next to them was closed also, and I asked a waiter who had just gotten off if there were any places open late. He did not know any off the top of his head, but then remembered Applebee's. Right on the other side of the street was a Hardee's. They were open until 11. It was now 10:40, and I went in. I had driven nearly sixty miles down dark mountain roads just to have dinner, but to the person who survived the "Russian soda fiasco" and to someone who regularly drove the same distance from Oxnard to Manhattan Beach, this was worth it.

I got myself a chicken sandwich, then went to Walmart to get a toothbrush, and then drove the nearly sixty miles back to my hotel. I took a different route this time, one that was faster and less windy. At one junction, I made a right turn. Soon I saw a sign saying "Entering Bath County". Wasn't I supposed to be in Pocahontas County? Then I realized I had not only gotten to the wrong county, but to the wrong state- there was a welcome to Virginia sign! Luckily, I had only gone less than a mile off course and was able to immediately turn back around and get back to my now dark hotel, a hotel where a single light bulb was left on right outside my room to indicate where it was.

The following day, I took it easy, after having driven straight for seven days. I was to stay for three nights at this hotel, possible a fourth night. That first morning it was raining and quite cold. I went to the hotel's lobby and told the people who were there that morning about my electrosensitivity and that I was thinking of moving there. They told me that a lot of people were moving there for that reason. Breakfast was served at the hotel that day, a hearty one of French toast and fruit, At the table, I met another couple staying at the hotel and they told me they also had delays the previous night and did not get to the hotel until 10 PM. I told them and the Utahn about my misadventures from the previous night and how I had to drive to Lewisburg to get dinner.

After breakfast, the Utahn introduced me to a woman named Casey working at the hotel who was also electrosensitive. Finally I was meeting someone else who not only was concerned about electromagnetic radiation, but felt the same way as I felt and who was aware of her condition. She told me that she had always been sensitive to high tension electric poles. Like me, her condition had gotten worse with the advent of wireless technology, and it got to the point where she could barely get out of bed. Then that past July she and her family came to Pocahontas County on vacation and she realized she was feeling much better. As such, they went back home, sold their things, and moved to West Virginia. As soon as she moved there, her condition improved. She now could function regularly and told me she kept getting better. She lived in a camper on the hotel's property and told me she might eventually buy a house.

Casey lived with her husband and preteen daughter, who was being homeschooled. I asked her how was it for her daughter to move there. She told me that it was an adjustment, but that she still had friends coming to her place on a regular basis. To me, this was a good sign. The girl was not from there, did not talk like native West Virginians, yet people were still nice enough to become her friends. I asked Casey if her daughter missed having a phone. She told me that she would draw a lot and never had a cell phone, but that her older children who did not live with her were lost on their phones.

Living in a camper was not for me. Plus, driving one all the way to West Virginia would be too complicated. I would need to find either an apartment or a house. The problem was that there were no rentals in Green Bank. While there were some good quality houses for around 200 000, neither I and especially not my father wanted to buy a house there before I had lived there long enough to know that that was where I wanted to stay. I asked the Utahn for advice and he told me I should contact someone named Jessica who was very active with the electrosensitive community, and that she sometimes would rent out rooms in her house. I asked him if she was the woman who appeared on a lot of international TV programs and he told me that was the one. I asked him if she did not live in a backwoods cabin, as was shown in the programs in which she appeared. He told me that she did have that cabin, but most of the time she lived in a regular house on the main road through Green Bank. He told me that he would e-mail her to schedule an appointment for me to meet her.

I then went to the hotel's two story library. I was checking out their movie collection and the Utahn was there also. We talked about electrosensitivity and he told me that he was never aware of his condition before, but now he started noticing that even when going into Marlinton, which had cell service and where most businesses had wi-fi, he would start getting sleepy. I think that all people are sensitive to electromagnetic radiation to some extent, because it interferes with the way our bodies work, but because we are so much surrounded by it and so attached to technology, most of us do not notice our sensitivities, and it is only when you are removed from these pollutants that you start noticing mow much better you feel without them. The Utahn told me he was trying to establish a mindful living community near the hotel, which I found to be a great idea. I told him I might want to join that community.

I took a nap in my room afterwards, but could not fall asleep. At 2 PM, with the rain gone, I left my hotel and headed out to Green Bank proper. I drove down Highway 92 counting down the miles to Green Bank. It was very exciting to be heading to that place that I had read so much about over the past eight years but that I was unable to go to before. Soon I was driving down the main road of Green Bank, population 143, with its gas station, the Dollar General, the senior center, a couple churches, and the payphone in the gas station parking lot that was regularly shown in the media but which was out of service at the moment. There was also a wellness center, a sign that health conscious people were indeed moving there. I drove past the library that did not have wi-fi and was a popular gathering spot for the electrosensitives. That was when I finally got to see the large radio telescope, of which there was a clear view from the library's lawn. I was going to use the computers in the library, but then decided to go have lunch and come back later.

I drove six miles from Green Bank to the historic railroad town of Cass, a touristy place known for its rail excursions. I went into one of two restaurants there and ordered a steak sandwich. This was essentially a country store with a lunch counter- every small village in West Virginia had one, and this one sold a few fancier items such as artisanal honey and chocolates. While walking around the store, a guy with Down Syndrome was coming up to me trying to hug me, at which point I told him not to do that.

When I sat down to eat, there was a woman sitting near me wearing a shirt reading "Unborn lives matter". Seeing how much support there was for anti-abortion legislation in some states and billboards supporting so-called "heartbeat bills" was a culture shock for me coming from California and reading magazines largely critical of these measures. I soon heard that woman talking with the woman who took my order about places she was thinking of traveling to. Once they were done talking, I told the Unborn Lives Matter woman about my trip and that I was thinking of moving to that area because of my electrosensitivity. She was on her iPad when I first walked in. That restaurant had wi-fi, as most businesses there did, even the ones close to the observatory. However, once I told her that I was electrosensitive, she got off. We got into a long conversation about traveling and her son- she was the mother of the person with Down Syndrome. She told me that she liked to travel but did not know how her son would be treated in different places. I told her to travel to blue states. When she scoffed at that idea, I told her that in those places people will at least pretend to like her son. Then I asked her how did her son get treated locally and she told me that people who knew him treated him very well, and that the people in that area tended to be very nice. I asked her if they would be accepting and she told me that they would. Later on her husband came in. He was originally from Baltimore, but had lived in West Virginia for the past forty years and told me he would never want to live in Baltimore again.

I later asked the woman if anyone ever criticized her over her politics. She told me that these things did not usually bother people there. Even though I was very much pro choice, I did not want to start a whole argument with her. I was tired of the cancel culture and the judgmentalness people can have towards others with opposing political views. I wanted a place where people were just respectful of one another and, most of all, nice. That woman was very nice. She loved her disabled son. She liked talking to others. Even her shirt suggested that, while she did not hold the same views as me, she did very much care about the weaker of us. I also liked how she drove her son on a regular basis from the town fifteen miles away where they lived to Cass so that he could interact with the woman at the restaurant and for her to give him all the hugs he wanted. Even if not everyone was open to hug him, there was one person at the store who was.

This reminded me of how I would drive a long distance to the Manhattan Beach stores. Some people would criticize me for doing that, saying that those people were at the stores to work, but here was another person with a disability doing just that and having the best time when he was there.

After lunch, I went across the river to see the main part of Cass. I stopped at the train depot with its gift shop and restaurant before driving down the main street with its whitewashed identical cabins that used to house railroad workers but were now part of a state park. Where the town ended there was a fire station and a girl was standing outside, lo and behold, on her cell phone. There was also smartphone use and wi-fi in and immediately around the train depot, but the good thing was that between these two ends of town there was no connectivity. As such, when walking among the railroad cabins, as I did after driving back around, I did not need to worry about people near me being on their devices. Some of the cabins were open, and I thought they were being kept as museums of the way the railroad workers lived, but when I walked into one of them, I saw it had a flat screen TV. I inquired at the train station and was told that these were all rental cabins. I thought they might be good places for me to stay if coming to the area for a month or more, but they were a bit expensive and the longest they could be rented out was two weeks.

I then went back to the Green Bank Library. While it was a main hangout spot for the electrosensitive community, it was not conducive to socializing- the people there were busy on the computers with the wired Internet or reading books. I went on a computer there to check my e-mail and do a couple other things. When logging on to Facebook, I saw Jessica was one of the recent users on that computer. I had been seeing her posts for years and was excited to actually be using a computer that she was regularly using. I posted on Facebook that I finally made it to Green Bank and would soon get many likes.

When I was done with the library, I drove down to Marlinton for dinner. I made it a point to get there before the restaurants closed, and I got there right before 6 PM- with plenty of time to spare. I walked into the Italian restaurant in town after seeing advertisements for it at my hotel. There were several people on their devices there, so I decided to check out another place that maybe did not have wi-fi or otherwise a crowd that would use it. That place also had several people on their devices and was quite busy, so I decided I would come back to the Italian place later. I walked into the main grocery store before going back to the restaurant at 6:30, by which time there were fewer people there. The food was not very authentic or gourmet as would be expected in some other parts of the country- it was "Italian food in West Virginia" as one person described it. But the food was not bad either and was still tasty. I especially liked the waitresses over there. They were warm and nice to talk to, and they told me to come back again. I told them that I was thinking of moving there because of my electrosensitivity, and even if there might have been people on their devices there, they told me that that was a good place for that. They told me that in that area, even with reception, people would usually only go on their cell phones because they needed to. They would not just go on them to spend time on them. Indeed, cell phone use there was less than in California.

I met up with Jessica the following morning. I drove to her beautiful house in Green Bank, making sure beforehand there were no dogs. There were none, and Jessica did not allow renters to bring them in either. I met a woman named Hillary who had just moved to Green Bank two days prior and who was renting a room from her. I told Jessica that I had seen her on so many TV programs and documentaries from Israel, Australia, and many other places. Indeed, there was a lot of information about Green Bank and electrosensitivity in international media, and when at my hotel I was asked where I found out about them I told them they appeared on a German website. American media tends to shy away from talking about these things, in large part because of the advertisement money from the phone and tech industries. Jessica and I talked about a couple of Israeli activists against electromagnetic radiation and how it seemed like many openly electrosensitive people were Israeli. I have several theories as to that. Israelis tend to have high intelligence, so they would be aware of these things. Israel was one of the first places to have heavy cell phone use, so that means more time for people to have developed sensitivities. Its population is dense, so its citizens have very few places to escape the radiation. Furthermore, Israelis and their ancestors have for centuries resisted conquest by the Egyptians, Babylonians, Persians, Greeks, Romans, Nazis, and Arabs, so the ones who are electrosensitive are resisting conquest by the phone and tech industries. However, these constitute only a small fraction of Israelis- most of them are addicted to their devices and use them a lot.

If I just wanted to get away from electromagnetic radiation, I did not need to go all the way to West Virginia. There were many empty places in the West that I could go to that would be much closer to Los Angeles. However, I also wanted a place with people, and for a community of people who did not use cell phones or wi-fi you needed to travel farther. There was a similar community near Snowflake, Arizona that had very little electromagnetic radiation and a good number of electrosensitives. However, that place was more geared toward multiple chemical sensitives. While I also have a mild form of that condition, as many electrosensitives do, the people in the Snowflake community have a severe form. These people can be sensitive to the slightest speck of dirt on one's clothing, and for someone who already has difficulties in socializing I do not need another reason for people to shun me. Jessica also had some multiple chemical sensitivity, and picked up some chemicals from my jacket, but in her case we went and sat outside and she was fine.

We talked for more than an hour about politicians not addressing the radiation problems and that they were being corrupted by the multitrillion dollar phone and tech industries. Furthermore, she believed that some of the politicians who did speak about these issues might be agents for the phone industry who were trying to do damage control. She as well as others who have appeared in the media did not like how the media portrayed them in ways they considered negative. Jessica, for example, was a very normal, if somewhat hippie-ish, person despite her sensitivities. She was not the backwoods hermit that some programs made her out to be. She was also concerned about upcoming wireless technologies, especially Elon Musk's Starlink satellites that would eventually beam wireless Internet down from space to every corner of the Earth. She said that they might also bring it down to Green Bank and decide to shut down the observatory. I told her that I did not think that would happen. If the corporations would force wi-fi on ones who moved to a certain corner of the world to avoid it, they would seem tyrannical, and as powerful and deep pocketed at these corporations are, they would not want to seem tyrannical.

As Jessica was telling me all this, I was noticing the birds and crickets chirping out in the fields, organisms that were dying out in much of the rest of the world and for which electromagnetic radiation has been blamed. Jessica also told me that twenty years prior she had a severe stomach disease where she dropped to 77 pounds, but ever since she moved to Green Bank she was in good health. I myself was feeling much healthier in Green Bank. I no longer had the migraines or the body aches I was experiencing in California and it was much easier for me to talk to people. I thought of telling Jessica about my Asperger's, but I did not. As that moment when I was sitting with her, I felt that my Asperger's was much less serious and that I did not even need to mention it. I just very much hoped my parents would be supportive of my moving there.

The one thing I did not like about some of the electrosensitives was that they were pessimistic. This pessimism was found among many different types of activists and I did not see it as a good thing. It only breeds unhealthy anger and depression and turns more moderate people away. True, some of the greatest positive movements in the world were born out of anger, but not all activists are comfortable being around angry people and there is a way to do it without anger. I say that people should be aware of the situation and the risks, but also be hopeful. Be hopeful but do not give up the fight.

After meeting with Jessica, I spent some time with Hillary helping her move a table. I spent some time with her hearing her life story. She told me she was not a very social person, but was nevertheless nice and told me she would like to go on a hike with me if I moved there. I told her that I do not like dogs, as I did not want her to bring one when we would hike. She was very much of a dog person- the only reason she did not have one now was because Jessica would not allow one in her house. She did, however, tell me she would not bring a dog when hiking with me.

After meeting with Jessica and Hillary, I went back to Highway 66 (not historic U.S. 66- that one never passed through West Virginia), but instead of stopping in Cass I continued to the ski resort of Snowshoe. Past Cass the road went in steep switchbacks up the forested fall colored mountain. Snowshoe is at 4800 feet above sea level, more than 2000 feet higher than Green Bank, and a good place to go to in the summer, I thought, should Green Bank get too hot and sweaty. It is somewhat unique for a ski resort with the town situated at the top of the mountain rather than at the base. That place did have wi-fi and cell reception. Even though the radiation was much less than where I lived, after having spent time in the largely EMF free environments of my hotel and Green Bank I felt the radiation more intensely now and started getting a bit dizzy. Also, none of the restaurants and stores were open there this time of year. Had they been open, I could have gone to eat there my first night and it would have been much closer than Lewisburg.

I continued on to the town of Elkins, fifty miles from Green Bank and with 7700 people the largest town in the vicinity. I walked into a store by the railroad depot that the tourist train from Cass reaches, half expecting to see a large unleashed dog there, but there was none. West Virginia has one of the highest number of dogs per capita in the United States, but neither in West Virginia nor anywhere on my trip as of yet did I see dogs all over the place like I did in California. Dogs being taken into stores and restaurants is more of west coast thing. It is also the case in Colorado. In some East Coast cities one finds many people walking their dogs. But that is not the majority of the United States. In much of the country, dogs are still treated as animals and not as children. As such, they are kept in people's yards and homes, taken on hunts, but they are not going to be found in public buildings either and as such the environment will be much easier for me.

I drove back to Green Bank and the library to check my messages. Then I went to the convenience store by the gas station where there was a food stand. For their special they had a fajita sandwich. I was quite surprised to see that on the menu given that that small town had very few, if any, Hispanics. The fajita sandwich was not what a purist Mexican would consider authentic, but it was nevertheless tasty- much more tasty than what one would expect from a gas station convenience store.

Back at the hotel, I met some more people now. The hotel's librarian was there with her children and Casey was also there with her husband and daughter. All of them seemed very nice and respectful people, and they all told me they liked living there. They told me that in the East Coast places that they came from the people were not nearly as nice and that they always had to worry about their children being harmed by others, but that that was not the case in the neighborly area where they lived now. There the children could safely play, interact with others, and go to places without a cell phone- all without their parents worrying too much about them (though they still worried when their children did not tell them where they were going, as was the case that night with the librarian's son). And no one at the hotel that day was checking their phones when sitting at the table- the wi-fi was not turned on. This was an affirmation for me that not only was this a place where some older people go to escape technology, but where the next generation was also being raised to not be too attached to technology. This was very important to me, because it ensures that the more technology free lifestyle that I and some other people want will not die out. I was now more convinced that this was the place for me.

The following morning I went on a tour of the Observatory, which I did not get to do the previous two days as it was closed. We got to see the various telescopes up close, including the humongous Robert C. Byrd telescope, the landmark of Green Bank and at 100 meters in diameter the world's largest fully steerable telescope. The dish is supposed to be circular, but it was not quite built as one. It was assembled by placing long rectangular metal strips next to each other, so the end result looks like a heavily pixilated circle on an old computer program. These telescopes are sensitive to electronics even when they are not wireless. As such, no trucks with modern electronic engine starters may service the telescopes- the observatory maintains a fleet of old diesel trucks. And neither are digital cameras allowed by the telescopes. The gift shop sells disposable film cameras, of which I got one. Our guide, a transplant from England, told us about the work done at the observatory. Some of this included witnessing the formation of new stars through the faint radio signals these events give out.

Supposedly 20 percent of their funding was for searching for extraterrestrials. The observatory was in financial trouble a few years back and had many people, both scientists and the electrosensitives, concerned about its possible demise. Fortunately, private investors were able to keep the funds going and the observatory now operates as the Green Bank Observatory, no longer a part of the National Radio Astronomy Observatory that operates similar sites in New Mexico and Chile.

After the tour, I ate at the cafeteria. I talked to the woman working at the gift shop as well as to someone from San Diego who told me his electrosensitive wife wanted to move there. There were crowds of people at the visitor center, but I realized I did not need to worry, or to avoid places there because there was a line. While most electronic equipment is allowed at the visitor center, there still was no wireless reception that people could use to irradiate me. Even if people did take out their phones, they could only use them to look at things that were already downloaded.

Later that afternoon I went back to the library to look at houses online. I was not sure at first whether I wanted to see houses on this trip, but now that I was seriously thinking of moving there, I decided to check out some places. I got the addresses from the Internet, but when I tried finding the streets by map, I could not find them. The roads had different names on the maps than they did in the listings! I finally found the locations of two houses that had maps for them on the realtor's website and I drove to them. The first one was relatively easy to find, but I only found it thanks to the signs pointing to the house- the street sign was quite well hidden. The final street leading to the house was unpaved, so I was not sure if that was something I wanted, but once I got to the house it did look nice. The second house was more difficult to find. I was driving down a back road in Appalachia looking for it, wondering if the 6/2 road down which I was driving was the one named Kensington, but I could not find the house.

I met up with the real estate agent the following morning at the gas station in Green Bank. He would lead me to the houses that I did not find. I told him that I did find that one house down the unpaved road and that I was not sure that I wanted it. He told me that it should not matter that it was on an unpaved road, as these roads would still be safe to drive. Then he suggested that I get a 4x4 vehicle, which West Virginians tended to have. I looked around me and did see a lot of 4x4s, but there were also a lot of regular cars, a fact I pointed to my agent. He told me that if you are not going to drive in the snow a regular car is fine, but otherwise you should get a 4x4. I was certainly not going to let myself get stuck in the snow, especially not when the lights go off. When my electricity went out in the Ventura County wildfires of 2017, I went to a hotel where there was power.

I visited four houses that day, especially liking one newly built house with rich wood panelings. I had to tell the realtor that I was not ready to buy yet but that I just wanted to look to see what I might want. My plan was now to come back to Green Bank, get a rental for a couple months, get to know the scene to make sure it is not another unfriendly Oregon that only appears friendly at first glance, and if I still liked it after a couple months buy something there. I did not really want to rent a room in someone's house, but I was told that I could stay at the hotel long term and get a discount. That was my plan now.

By 1:45 I was done seeing the houses and was now off to New Jersey and my aunt. I was disappointed to leave Green Bank, as soon I would be back in the world of cell towers, smartphones, and the headaches and pains they would give me and that were absent in Green Bank. I left Green Bank with a sense that this was the place for me. About ten years of my life had gone to waste being exposed to electromagnetic radiation and running away from it- time that I could have used to develop a career or my writing talent but which I was never able to achieve to the fullest.

There was another thing I liked about West Virginia- the people. This was a place where people were much more friendly than in all of the places in the West that I checked out. Maybe not so much Green Bank but West Virginia in general was like that. This was a place where people helped each other when in need. This was a place where crime was below average and where people did not worry about social ills such as sex trafficking and mass shootings. Even though these things can unfortunately happen anywhere, the people in the small towns of West Virginia were justified in not worrying about these things as much as people in other more central and less community oriented places. And it goes both ways. Because there is less crime, people are more willing to help each other out. Because people look out for each other more there is less crime.

West Virginia did have some unusual looking people, both in their appearances and in their gazes, but I liked that- as I can be unusual looking in these things also. I always found it offensive when these types of people were portrayed as the bad people in made for TV movies, just as nonwhites find negative portrayals of their people as offensive. Here, however, I was surrounded by people who one could say looked a bit unusual, and people did not think negatively of them or not worthy of being befriended. In fact, looking a bit unusual here was normal.

I no longer missed Manhattan Beach as I did when I moved to Oregon. While there were still a few people there whom I greatly liked, I no longer had any illusions about that place. I did not want to go back to a place where people pretended to want to get lunch with me but did not really want to. I did not want to go back to a place where people were constantly on their phones and where they liked dogs more than people. There was only one thing that greatly worried me now, and justifiably so- that my parents would try to stop me.

V.   With my aunt

I drove nearly three hours through the mountain valleys of West Virginia from Green Bank until I crossed into the western part of Maryland. From there I took two historic highways- the National Road, the first major highway in the United States with paving, and the Pennsylvania Turnpike, the first long distance limited access highway in the United States. My drive went well, but as I got into the big city environment of Philadelphia, I again began getting the headaches of the electromagnetic radiation. Nevertheless, the drive was still exciting for me when I drove over the Ben Franklin Bridge into New Jersey and the suburbs where my aunt lived. I had gone on those roads several times before when visiting my aunt, but never had I gone on them after coming from California by car all the way. I was now trying to remember the tricky diagonal roads needed to get to the large complex where her townhouse was located.

This aunt was someone I was very close to, even when she still lived in Israel. Then when she moved to New Jersey, she wanted to spend more time with me. Problem was that by then she had little kids. They visited Los Angeles right after the move when the girl was not quite four and the boy not quite two. One day we spent the afternoon at the university where my mother taught. On the way back, I thought we were only going to drop them off at my uncle's where they were staying, but instead we spent an hour in the car in traffic giving my aunt a tour of Beverly Hills and Fairfax while the kids were at their crankiest. I could not bear it and when we stopped for an early dinner I called my dad to pick me up. It was at that moment at age seventeen that I decided once and for all I never want to have children.

A year after that incident, my aunt began telling me that her kids were more mature and that she wanted me to come visit them, but when they came to visit us they seemed even more hyper than the previous time. I came with my parents to visit when her children were four and six, but we stayed in a hotel and I would only spend very little time around the kids. Other than that, I would only see my aunt when she could be away from them. One day I spent all day sightseeing around Philadelphia and the Amish Country with my father and did not arrive at my aunt's house until 9 PM. When we got there, my aunt told me that the girl was very excited about our visit and that she kept waiting for us to arrive, but she had just gone to sleep before we got there. I decided that was not very nice to do. I told my aunt to wake her up, especially since she was the cool and calm one of the siblings, but my aunt did not want to. Soon, however, the energetic boy did get up to see us.

My aunt kept asking me to come back without my parents after that visit, but I told her not until they would be preteens and truly mature. True to my word, I did come back to New Jersey in 2008 when my cousins were ten and twelve. On that trip I took them to Baltimore and showed them the place where The Star Spangled Banner was written. I also went then to New York to visit my college friend Isabel.

Despite my cousins having grown into intelligent teenagers and then adults, I hadn't been to New Jersey since 2010, not since I stopped flying. I was happy to be back there now. I got to my aunt's place at 9:45, a bit late but they still waited for me for dinner. My aunt was indeed a good cook and over the four days I stayed at her place, she cooked dinners for me that I liked so I would not need to go to restaurants. I also did not need to go to a hotel, as I had my male cousin's room available with him being off at college.

As soon as I walked into the door, it was evident this was a very traditional Jewish home. There were mezuzahs as every doorway and hamsas seemingly all over the place. My aunt kept kosher and separated meat from dairy. My mother sometimes would question my aunt over why she had recently become so much like that, but on this visit I decided many of us have certain ways of doing things due to concerns that are important for us but not for others. What my aunt was with meat and dairy was what I was with wi-fi.

I made her wireless house more wired while I was there. I plugged in a corded phone that my aunt got for me. I ran an Ethernet cable from the modem to an old PC that my aunt's family no longer used. The lost bag from Utah had arrived at her place so I had the cable to connect. I did not turn off the wi-fi, as my aunt's husband needed it for his job. Nevertheless, I did move the modem farther from my bedroom.

The following day, the girl cousin Daphna drove us to New York to visit Yoav, the other cousin. On the way there, I realized that it had been exactly twenty years to the day since my aunt moved from Israel. Now she was not sure whether to celebrate or to mourn, as she did not like life in the United States too much. Being a very proud Israeli, she always thought that would be a better place for me. I indeed did think of moving there on occasions. The people there were warm and social. People were willing to help each other out. I would be surrounded by a lot of family. However, it was also a foreign culture to me, even though I had grown up in an Israeli household and had been to Israel nine times. People there could also be judgmental, and her notion of Israelis being better than Americans was largely due to a cultural bias. People there had lots of children, and little kids were more out in the open than in the United States. Also, if you are looking for a place with low cell phone use and affordability, Israel is not the place. Most Israelis are on their phones a lot, despite the few active electrosensitives. And as I was told by a different cousin who moved to Israel, if you move there, you need to learn to live with less, as most things there are more expensive, and some are not even as widely available as in the United States.

As soon as we were over the George Washington Bridge, I had made it from Manhattan to Manhattan. While I was not the one driving, I did not care too much. I had driven all the past eleven days and my aunt wanted to give me a break. Also, I had driven in Manhattan on my 2008 trip and driving there is not for the faint of heart- there are pedestrians all over the place and taxis stopping right in the middle of the street. The good thing about driving there is that the grid pattern and the numbered streets make it easy to find one's way around. As I told Isabel when I easily found her place there, I knew 111th street would be right next to 112th.

Yoav studied at Columbia and lived in that same neighborhood by the campus where Isabel used to live, but a few blocks farther up. I liked that part of New York. It was still Manhattan, but not nearly as crowded as places farther down like Times Square. The trees on the streets were beautiful against the brick apartment buildings. I went up into my cousin's apartment. It felt very much like a small artist's apartment in the city- which it essentially was, except that it was shared by four college students. I met my cousin's roommates and friends, all of whom were very nice.

We went to lunch at a nearby Ethiopian restaurant, meeting up with the daughter of my aunt's best friend from Israel, who was now living in New York as an au pair and whom I hadn't seen since I was in Israel in 2008 when she was ten. After lunch, Yoav showed me around Columbia. Then we went to a bakery on Amsterdam Street. I did not go inside, as it was too crowded for me, so I went on a walk with my aunt. We walked down the 111th Street where Isabel used to live, and right past her old apartment. We went to the beautiful Riverside Park, where my aunt kept having to sit down and where I kept walking away to avoid the dogs. My aunt told me that these poor dogs were just trying to come up to me and I wouldn't let them.

I wanted to walk without pausing much. It was easier to avoid dogs that way and I also wanted to cover more ground in less time, and not to get to places I wanted to go and find out they were closed. I was not so much bothered by my aunt having to stop occasionally to rest, but I was bothered by her constantly wanting to take my pictures to send to my mother. Even if she were going to put it on airplane mode and only send the pictures when stepping away from me, I did not want that. I did not want my mother following me around when I was on vacation. As such, my aunt and I soon parted ways.

I walked rather fast toward Grant's Tomb. Around 1900, this was one of New York City's most popular attractions, with Civil War veterans coming there in droves to pay their respects to the general under whom they fought, but as these solders died out the site fell into obscurity. It is now one of the city's lesser attractions- a beautiful neoclassical mausoleum in which the 18th U.S. President is buried, surrounded by a well landscaped park. I arrived there fifteen minutes before closing, walking around the basement rotunda where Grant and his wife are entombed. Earlier on this trip, I passed by the house in Point Pleasant, Ohio, where Grant was born. He was now the third president of whom I visited both his birthplace and gravesite (Richard Nixon and Lyndon Johnson were the others). My college tourism professor had been to the ones of every President.

After Grant's Tomb, I was getting a bit tired from walking also and headed back to Yoav's apartment. I figured that my aunt did not spend much more time sitting on park benches as I did at the mausoleum and that if she wasn't at my cousin's place now she would be there soon. I was very tired from standing up by the time I got to the apartment, but fortunately someone who was exiting the building opened the door soon, and I sat on a bench in the lobby waiting for my aunt. After about ten minutes, I decided to go up to the apartment to see what was going on. I knocked on the door and the roommates answered. My cousin had returned early to study, but was now lying in bed. He called my aunt and she said she was at the bookstore at 116th and Broadway and asked that I go meet her there. Then when I left the apartment, I was told to meet her at 116th and Riverside.

I did not feel like walking the six blocks back to 116th and then back to the apartment and the car, but I figured it was not a big deal. I went to 116th and Riverside, but I did not see any bookstore there, so I went to Broadway. The bookstore was at 115th street and it was the one for Columbia. I went in there, but my aunt was not there. Now I was really tired from walking so I took a taxi back to Yoav's. When I arrived there, I asked my cousin, still in bed, to call my aunt to tell her to just meet me at the apartment. She and the rest of her family got there about fifteen minutes later and my aunt told me that she called my name when I was at 116th and Riverside. I told her that I did hear someone calling my name but I did not see her, and that I did not expect her to just be at the corner and not at the bookstore. My aunt now apologized for not having stayed with me.

It was now after 6 PM, dusk, and I felt that much of my day had been wasted both looking for my aunt and waiting around for my family. I wanted to see more of the city while I was there, especially the 9/11 Memorial that I had never been to. I had been there in 2002 right after the towers fell, but that was long before the formal memorial was placed. I asked Daphna if she could drive us there, and we all went. Had this been pre-smartphones, I would have taken the subway. However, public transportation is now not too different from airplanes with crowds of people on their wireless devices, so now that is also a no go for me.

There was a lot of traffic heading to the other end of Manhattan, and there was no easy parking at the memorial- Daphna had to drive around while the rest of us got out- but it was worth it. Here was where a major tragedy happened not too long ago, but where a park had beautifully risen from its ashes. This tree lined place in the shadow of the Freedom Tower and other tall buildings was now a huge gathering spot for the city, but one where the waterfalls made out of the foundation holes of the Twin Towers showed that the tragedy has not been forgotten.

The following day it was raining, but I still wanted to go out and explore Philadelphia. My aunt did not really want to go out, but agreed to go with me granted that we would stay indoors. I drove this time- my aunt was not too comfortable with driving in the rain. But as it turned out, she was not too comfortable riding in the rain either, after having been in a major car crash five years earlier. So five minutes after we left she asked me to drop her off at her friend's place.

I continued into the city alone. I parked in the historic section of Philadelphia to walk around, not being bothered by the rain, which was not too strong now. I walked past the old Quaker meeting house, outside of which now stood an LGBTQ pride sign. Similar signs stood elsewhere in the area. That part of Philadelphia might be ancient, but it is very much of a living community where institutions established more than 300 years ago and dedicated to tolerance and equality still promote these issues in their contemporary guises in front of their ancient buildings.

Soon after, the rain stopped, and now the sun came out. The temperature was in the low 70s now, but even though I was wearing shorts- a decision I made when

I looked at the weather forecast and which startled my aunt and her doctor husband- it felt significantly warmer. This was the east coast where humidity was high and the slightest bit of heat caused one to sweat. I was now wondering whether this was a part of the country I really wanted to move to. West Virginia would not get as hot in the summer as Philadelphia, but it would still get hotter than this and there was a reason why I never went to the East Coast in the summer.

I quickly returned to my car and now drove around the various neighborhoods of the city. I drove north on Third Street past the original Colonial center and into the neighborhood a few blocks north called Northern Liberties. This was one of the first suburbs of Philadelphia, and before it and other suburbs consolidated with Philadelphia in 1854 Northern Liberties was one of the ten largest cities in the United States. This was clearly a gentrifying neighborhood, one where postmodern apartment buildings were going up among the old brick ones. At first I was thinking to myself that this is a tragedy they are tearing down the old buildings, but soon I passed into a community that was not yet gentrified and where I understood why the new buildings in Northern Liberties had gone up- the old buildings were torn down a long time ago, and in the ungentrified neighborhoods these were still empty lots. I had seen this pattern of gentrification in Camden right before I crossed the river. The downtown saw new buildings go up and old ones being restored and/or upgraded, but the gentrification did not extend past downtown and the rest of the city was still full of poverty. I actually liked this type of gentrification better than the wholesale ones that happen in places like L.A. and New York. It beautifies a part of the city, and improves the whole city's reputation, but it also ensures that poor people still have a place to live.

I drove three miles north of Market Street before I became hungry and turned back around to South Philadelphia to go to Geno's, one of the landmark Philly steak places and a place I had never been to. I found it a bit overrated, but it is a Philadelphia classic and I had to try it. The building in Philadelphia I most wanted to see on this trip was not Independence Hall, not City Hall, and not the Mint- I had been to all these places on previous trips already. Rather, I wanted to go to Macy's, specifically the old Wanamaker's store in Downtown.

Every city in the United States at one time had its own downtown department store, with the big cities having multiple ones and the grander stores being very ornate. Many of these stores are gone now, largely due to changing tastes, declining downtowns, competition with big box stores, consolidations that took away the old local store nameplates (like Wanamaker's) and made them into

Macy's, and, more recently, online shopping. I was happy that Philadelphia still had an ornate downtown department store and was determined to see it now.

That Macy's was indeed very ornate, with its large eight story atrium and various arched panelings, among other architectural details. I told the workers that I was glad they still had that store. Generally century old department store buildings do not get torn down when the store closes. The building gets declared a historic landmark. But that only applies to the rather lackluster exterior- the interior often gets completely gutted as it is transformed to other uses. A few places are trying to prevent this practice, such as San Francisco which is requiring that when a large store around Union Square closes down the first three stories of the building that used to be retail be kept as such. Maybe forcing closing stores to be converted to other stores is not always economically viable in the age of Amazon, but I do like what San Francisco is doing with ensuring these buildings do not become gutted and that they remain open to the public. Any such ornate department store that closes should be made into restaurants, museums, or other uses where people will be able to walk in and see all the architecture of the old building.

That evening I went with my aunt to the house of an Israeli friend of hers. We talked about why I wanted to move to West Virginia and my concerns over wireless radiation. My friend's husband, who was on the other side of the argument, tried to reason with me. He told me in Hebrew "I know you're a smart guy. So tell me why is it that the whole world is attached to wireless devices and we are all still OK." I told him "Not everyone is still OK. Why do you suppose we have more cases of depression, suicide, autism, thyroid problems, and other things now? All these things have been linked to wireless radiation." That was when that guy decided there was no arguing with me and that I may be right. Then I asked the people in the room if their memory was less good now than it used to be, and all of them told me that it was less good. While some of the people in the room were old, one of them- my aunt's friend- was only forty- below the age where people are traditionally thought to begin losing memory. I did not ask my cousins that, as they were too little in the era before smartphones and wi-fi.

Despite acknowledging the harm that might be caused by this radiation, they still did not quite support my move to West Virginia. They asked me what would I do in such a place, and they did not want me leaving my parents behind to move there. I told them that I am very proud of my intellect and memory and would not let the phone and tech companies take that away from me just because they want to make money. When I was a child, I refused to take behavior modifying medications that might cause me to lose some of my talents. I would not let the corporations force such a drug upon me now, even if it meant that I would need to leave my parents or everything that I knew so that I could escape it.

The following day, I was scheduled to finish my drive to the Atlantic and to make it from coast to coast. I was supposed to meet with my old LMU friend Jen McQueen, who was now teaching at Monmouth by the Jersey Shore, and go with her to a pizza place in Asbury Park before taking a walk on the beach. However, when I woke up that morning, I had a Facebook message saying that she was feeling sick and that this was the first time in seven years she would miss a day at work, but she said she could still meet me for lunch if we did it closer to where she lived. Jen lived the next town over from Cherry Hill so I would be going to the coast on my own and decided to meet her at five after I was done.

At first I thought of simply somewhere on the Jersey Shore, but then when I saw New York was not too far and that there was not a lot of traffic on the way there and not a lot of traffic more in the outskirts of the city, I decided to go there instead. That way my drive would truly be Los Angeles to New York. I didn't need to drive to Manhattan, because I was just there two days prior- even if I was not the one driving, and also there was a Manhattan Beach in Brooklyn that could satisfy my Manhattan to Manhattan requirement. Rather I wanted to explore other parts of the city after never having been to the Outer Boroughs when not at JFK or on the highways.

I left my aunt's place at 11:20 that morning, wearing the T-shirt and socks from the volleyball tournament Hailey's family hosted on the Pacific beach where I met up with her to begin my journey thirteen days earlier. I put on my Neil Diamond CD as I headed down the New Jersey Turnpike to the beaches where he grew up.

An hour and a half later, I was on the Varrazano Narrows Bridge spanning New York Harbor. I was no longer listening to the Neil Diamond CD and now had the radio on. There came on Miley Cyrus's "The Climb", a song I thought was so symbolic for the occasion. I was climbing 200 feet up to the highest point on the roadway, and also, as the song sings about, I had finally achieved my goal despite all the obstacles that stood in the way. Now, after years of wanting to drive across the country, here I was driving from on this bridge after having driven from California and having a view of the tall buildings of Manhattan on one side and the buildings along New York's beaches on the other side, and beyond them my ultimate goal of the Atlantic.

I felt a bit nervous driving down the streets of New York once I got off the bridge, even though I had driven in the city that time in 2008. It was however not too different from driving in Los Angeles, especially in that less dense part of the city by the beach. My first stop was Coney Island. I walked on the boardwalk, which was nearly deserted, as it was a cloudy Monday and the amusement park had just closed for the season. I got a hot dog at the landmark Nathan's and was happy to not have a long line. There was the beach there, but I did not want to make it my final destination. The beach there is technically on a bay of the Atlantic and I wanted to make it more to the open ocean, which would be at Rockaway. Plus, I wanted to fill up my bottle of Atlantic Ocean water farther from the polluted New York Harbor.

I continued on, down through the next community of Brighton Beach. I was familiar with that name from Neil Simon's play and movie that I saw as a child- a neighborhood that was now full of immigrants and restaurants from the former Soviet Union. The next community was the one whose name I most liked- Manhattan Beach. Then it was off to the Rockaway Peninsula. Though there was only a small bridge, it was a nearly five dollar toll- the third of five tolls I had to pay that day and one of the most annoying things about driving in New York. I continued on to the main part of Rockaway, taking a couple of detours due to construction. Once I got to 91st Street, I decided that is the farthest east I would go and I turned toward the beach.

It took me another five minutes to get to the beach, even though it was only two blocks away. I could not cross the railroad tracks on 91st street even though it was an elevated track, so I had to get back to the main road, where I had a very long wait to turn left. But finally I made it to the beach. I parked across the street from it, heading back to my car once I realized I forgot my Tropicana bottle to use to collect the water, and then went back, this time really to the beach. I stood on the raised boardwalk looking down at the beach and the shrub covered dunes that were familiar to me from some movies, and at the long tall beachfront buildings on the shore. This place looked like a cross between New York and Long Island, and was technically in both. Above me were the airplanes making their final approach to JFK. I was thinking of all the times I was looking down at that beach when flying into that airport in the pre wi-fi era, whether it was to continue to Israel or to visit the city, and never did I imagine someday I would be driving to that beach all the way from Los Angeles.

Now it was time to go down to the beach itself. I waited for someone walking her dog to go by. Then there was a bicyclist running his unleashed dog on the boardwalk and I had to yell at him "Make sure that the dog does not come up to me!" before I climbed on top of a bench (the dog stayed away from me). Then, with the other dog on the beach gone, I went down. I dipped my feet and hands in the water, filled up my bottle, and now I had really made it. Los Angeles to New York. Manhattan to Manhattan. Pacific to Atlantic. Across the country.

There were more places in Brooklyn and Queens that I wanted to explore. There was the TWA Hotel built into the restored architecturally significant terminal that I flew into so many times when that airline was still in operation. There was the Hasidic turned hipster neighborhood of Williamsburg. But it was now 2:30 and I did not want to risk getting caught in traffic after visiting these places. Also, I wanted to make it in time to see Jen McQueen. As such, I was satisfied with having visited Coney Island and Rockaway, and especially with achieving my coast to coast goal.

I made it back to Cherry Hill at 4:30, not having too much traffic. I drove around looking for the restaurant Jen told me to meet her at. It was a bit hard to find in the sea of large shopping centers along Highway 70, but I did ultimately find it. Jen arrived a few minutes late, appearing quite sick. I was happy that she did not bail on me and that I did not miss seeing her the only time I might be in New Jersey for a long time. She also showed me how committed of a person she was when most of my friends in Southern California would cancel on me even if they were a little unwell, or even just a little tired. As she put it, she was East Coast, and if she said she would be somewhere she would be there.

The stereotype about unfriendly New Yorkers and New Jerseyites is true, but only when someone does not really like you or trust you. If they don't like you too much, they don't pretend they do, but if they like you they show it. While those mannerisms may mean fewer friendly interactions and more of the unfriendly ones, you also know who wants to be your friend and who doesn't, unlike in Southern California where it is not always easy to tell. Jen was a New Yorker who clearly liked me.

We talked about my trip that day and the things she was teaching in college. She also told me that she liked living near Philadelphia and liked it better than New York, which I found a bit surprising coming from someone who was always a proud New Yorker. She told me she liked Philadelphia more because it was a less congested city. Being a tourist, I still liked New York a bit more, because it had more to see and because it was New York. However, to live, Philadelphia is probably better. And I was sure glad I did not live in New York a few months later when it was struck hard by the pandemic.

I felt that I was wearing out my welcome at my aunt's place. Her husband was complaining that I was clogging the toilets by my heavy use of tissue paper and claimed that the wi-fi had stopped working (I moved the modem away from the room where I was sleeping, but did not disconnect it). As such, I was thinking of starting my trip back home that night. My aunt, however, was not bothered at all by these things and asked me to stay another night, which I did.

The following morning, I left after both my aunt and her husband went off to work. My aunt wanted me to give a presentation on my trip in her class, but the principal would not allow it. As such, I would need to just stop by and say goodbye to her. I drove to her Jewish school on my way out. I rang the door buzzer and was let in. I told the secretary I was there to see my aunt, but was told she was in class and could not come out. I left right then, but as soon as I got to my car I heard a knock on the window in front of me. I called out to my aunt, assuming it was her, but could neither near nor see through that window. I left right then, but when I called my aunt later, she told me that she had come out of the building to meet me and asked why did I not wait for her. I told her that I did not know it was she who banged on the window.

I liked how Green Bank was so close to my aunt where I could drive in one day to see her. I could easily go to her place for the holidays and have dinners with the guests. Only four hours away from me in Washington D.C. I had a cousin to whose place I could also go for the holidays. I was going to visit him on this trip but he was out of town. I had my uncle in Los Angeles who used to have holiday dinners, but his and his wife's old age and his recent stroke meant they would no longer be able to do that. Now if I would stay in Southern California it would only be my parents and I for the holidays, something that I found very depressing. It was a sign of the dysfunction my family had where we could not invite other guests. I needed a change of scenery.

VI.   Philadelphia Heading West

I was now off to Pittsburgh, where I would be spending the night. I drove back through Downtown Philadelphia, going down Market Street past the glass skyscrapers. Then I turned onto the old Lancaster Road, which took me right through West Philadelphia. I first passed through there in 1997 when I was on a trip with my parents. At that time, that area was full of gravely run down homes with broken windows. My parents told me they had never seen such deep poverty in the United States before and my father, not one to think of people living in such neighborhoods as necessarily harmless, was actually quite scared. On my drive there now, however, I came upon a different scene. The part of West Philadelphia right next to the universities and closest to downtown was now a nice multiethnic neighborhood. Farther west it was a bit more low income, but still a marked improvement over how it was in the 1990s. This is gentrification at its best. Areas become more livable and less crime ridden, but they do not become so cleaned up where the poor can no longer afford to live there. This is better than what I saw in Camden or North Philadelphia, because it was not only pockets that became highly gentrified with the rest of the area remaining essentially untouched. Rather the entire area was becoming just gentrified enough to make it a bit more livable. Some places farther west did remain quite run down, but nevertheless still a little less so than in the 1990s.

Past West Philadelphia, the transition to the wealthy neighborhoods at the city limits comes very fast. I drove through there and the upper middle class suburbs beyond, seeing the full spectrum of the Philadelphia area. I was going to continue on the Old Lancaster Road all the way through, but it was becoming a bottleneck of red lights and I was still in the middle of the metropolitan sprawl, so I soon got onto the freeway. The freeway paralleling the old road ends right past the suburban fringe and now I was back on the historic road to Lancaster. This was also part of the old Lincoln Highway, an early transcontinental automobile road running from New York to San Francisco.

A few miles before Lancaster one starts seeing the signs of Pennsylvania Dutch Country. I had been to that area several times before, driving on side roads that were shared by the Amish and their horse drawn wagons. I have long admired the Amish for their resistance to much of modern technology and the fact that they are still respected and allowed to live their lives in the 21st century. Some people suggested that I join the Amish, but I could not live without electricity or television either and their religion would be too strict for me.

I stopped for lunch at a buffet place on the highway. I was quite surprised that some of the young waitresses there were Amish, not expecting them to work at such places. I am not sure if they were full fledged Amish or just Mennonites, but there they were with their homemade clothes and bonnets. I hear many Amish now have their own businesses, needing the money from them for houses and land to house their growing population when land values are going up. Some of them even have cell phones now, but I doubt they are used for much else besides business, or that many Amish youth spend much of their day staring at smartphone screens.

Before Lancaster the highway is still nice, with farmland that is occasionally etched with rows of old houses along the highway. However, at the approach to the city the sprawl sets in- an endless parade of shopping centers filled with big box stores and restaurants and long waits at every traffic light. There is a freeway that goes around Lancaster, but it does not start until *after* the shopping centers. Indeed, after I got to the start of the old freeway, even though I remained on the old highway and was passing through a more central part of the city, my average speed increased.

On my 2008 visit to Philadelphia, I took my friend Erica, who was studying law at Villanova, on a day drive. When I brought her to Downtown Lancaster (my first time to the central part of the city), she asked me why were we going there. She told me that that place had nothing of interest, and not even a river for a nice waterfront. Then when I told her that I was trying to find the old highway, she told me that she did not think the original planners would be stupid enough to route the highway right through downtown if the traffic there would be that slow. Well, guess what Erica, they did. In the pre-automobile days, and even in the early automobile days, it was desired that a highway would pass right through the central part of the cities as to bring farm goods to the markets and to connect markets in one city to ones in other cities. It was only once automobiles became faster that slow speeds in the center of town became an issue and new roads were built on the outskirts of the towns. And Lancaster is a nice place to see. Granted it does not have nearly as much to offer as larger cities and does not have an especially scenic location, it still has some beautiful rows of 200 year old houses and brick buildings in its central area which make for a rewarding quick visit.

I was going to continue on the old highway through the charming town of Columbia and to the arched mile long bridge over the Susquehanna, but Erica was right, that highway was very slow, especially if I wanted to get to Pittsburgh that day. Plus, I already did that highway in 2008. As such, I turned to the freeway, having to sit through a couple long red lights on the outskirts of Lancaster before entering it.

Soon I was passing through York, another historic town that Erica complained I was taking her to. I was a bit brainwashed by her dislike of that place as I was driving on the newer freeway when on that road's passage along the northern part of the city the freeway ended and it became a multilane city road. Now there was again a succession of red lights with long waits, and I told myself that driving through the historic center would be so much nicer. As soon as I had the opportunity, I got on I-81 and exited on Market Street. Erica was again wrong. That town, like Lancaster, is a nice place to drive through. It also has neat rows of old houses and store buildings, and the town has some noteworthy history- it served as the capital of the U.S. for three months before Washington DC was built. And coming from a place where almost everything is new, at least from the past several decades, there is something about seeing rows of 200 plus year old buildings in cities in the East Coast and Europe and thinking that the towns in the area where I live were still small frontier backwaters or did not even exist at all at a time when these cities elsewhere were already sophisticated places.

The freeway ends right past York and now the old highway passing through the small towns was the main highway. The other time I was on that road was in 1997 when I went with my parents to Gettysburg. Though I was anxious to get to the famous battle site before sundown on that trip (we made it right after) and frustrated by the slow parts of the highway, I also even then when I was in ninth grade liked seeing the small towns with their squares and thinking that that is how people in some parts of the country live.

I did not need to see the battlefield again on this drive. I did nevertheless stop in Downtown Gettysburg to use the restroom. I found that small town to be a thriving place full of boutiques and was wondering why would a place in the middle of nowhere have all of this business just because it happens to be a Civil War battle site where Abraham Lincoln gave a famous speech that almost every American middle schooler studies. Then I realized there is more than history going on there- it is the site of Gettysburg College, a fairly prestigious school that actually predates the Civil War. I did see some of the battle site on this trip, passing by it along the highway right outside the city.

Driving west before sunset was not much of a problem this day, as the skies were overcast. However, a half an hour before sunset, as I was going up and down the ridges of the Alleghenies, there was a break in the clouds and the sun now shown in my eyes. Fortunately the road at this point did not always go west, turning north and south as it went up the mountain ridges, so I was mostly fine. I did nevertheless stop somewhere for a few minutes to wait for the sun to go behind a mountain ridge before continuing.

I got to the Pennsylvania Turnpike right at sunset and took that road for the remainder of my day's drive. Though that highway is also historic, it was nevertheless still another boring freeway. I spent the uneventful two hours on it counting down the miles to Pittsburgh except for one moment that I found very interesting. The main thing I associated with Pittsburgh was the 80s movie *Flashdance* that was set there and the catchy "What a Feeling" song from it. All throughout my drive that day and the night before, I was singing dum- dum dum dum- dum dum dum- dum dum dum- the opening notes. Then on my drive on the Turnpike, by an interesting coincidence, that song did come on the radio.

I got to my hotel in Downtown Pittsburgh at 8 PM, right across from the Three Rivers Stadium and with a view of the raised freeways. I went to eat at a sports themed restaurant near my hotel before going back to my room. The following day I gave myself a tour of this city with an extra H. I went to the park and point at the western end of downtown where the Allegheny and Monongahela Rivers meet to form the Ohio. Then I went across the rivers to the bluffs where Pittsburgh's famous incline reaches. The view from there was spectacular- with the central part of the city appearing a few hundred feet below and only the tallest downtown buildings rising above the level of the bluffs. I called the neighborhood on the bluffs the Hollywood Hills of Pittsburgh. While it was a nice area, it was much less ritzy than that part of L.A.

I drove around the various neighborhoods of the city that go up and down the hills, and down into the old boutique and restaurant lined thoroughfares at their base. Colin visited there the year before and considered moving there, liking how it resembled San Francisco but that it was much more working and middle class, and that despite some hard times in recent years with the closure of the steel mills, the place was now up and coming. One landmark of the city that I was interested in seeing was the Cathedral of Learning at the University of Pittsburgh. At 42 stories, this is the tallest university building in the western hemisphere.

Upon arriving at the building, my first impression was a cross between Los Angeles City Hall and a Gothic European cathedral. The building was meant to evoke the latter and the resemblance to the first is due to the fact that it is a tall building built in the same art deco period. I entered through the basement entrance on the street level and walked through the cavernous corridors of the building. I tried taking the elevators up to the higher floors, but they were a trick to use. I entered one and there were no buttons inside. It ended up taking me to the 20th floor. I got out there and realized that you needed to select your floor by pressing a keypad outside the elevator rather than inside it after you entered. This apparently made the elevators less crowded.

I had believed that every single floor of the building was decorated in a different theme representing a different historical/ cultural period. When I got up to the 20th floor, I saw that it looked just like a regular college office building. I now decided to go to the top floor to see the view from there. I tried typing in "42" and received an invalid floor massage. The highest I could get up in these elevators was the 35th floor. The first elevator that could get there I did not take, as there was someone inside on the cell phone. The next one also had someone inside so I did not take it. The third one, coming after being stuck on the 20th floor for ten minutes, did not have anyone inside so I took that one.

When I got to the 35th floor, I found myself in a two story library with some Gothic details. I took the stairs up to the next floor, which was more quiet, and took pictures of the dramatic view. Near me was a Chinese family who were with me on my first elevator ride (and who luckily were not on their phones). I talked to them now and they told me they had just moved to the states a year prior and wanted to finally visit this building in their neighborhood. I told them that I had read about in a tour book years earlier, where it was described as one of the great college buildings in the United States, and had wanted to see it ever since.

I asked the librarian about the themed floors and was told they did not have that but they did have are themed classrooms decorated in the styles of different nations, and that these were all on the first and third floors. I went down to the third floor, dodging multitudes of students on their devices, exploring these rooms. They tended to be quite embarrassing to visit, as all but two of them were functioning classrooms and most had students inside. Probably of greatest note there was the study commons. With its tall arched ceiling, it truly looked like the interior of a medieval cathedral in Europe, but was used for an American college building. I would have wanted to stay longer on the university's campus. I had at one time loved visiting universities, not only for their architecture, but because they are centers of learning filled with life and bright young minds. However, since smartphones and wi-fi became common, and with young college students being particularly attached to them, college campuses became one of the worst places for me to visit. I am very happy I went to college before these things became widespread.

When I got back home from my trip, my mom who is highly interested in Judaism asked me if I had visited any Jewish sites on the trip. I did not, though I did think of driving by the Tree of Life Synagogue in Pittsburgh, particularly since it had been almost exactly one year to the day since the mass shooting there. However, when I was in Pittsburgh, that did not cross my mind. I still had my long drive to Cincinnati that day and after a quick lunch of a Japanese crepe at a stand by the Cathedral of Learning I left the city.

I took the freeway out of Pittsburgh. Once I was in the town of Washington past Pittsburgh's suburbs, I got back off the freeway to take another stretch of U.S. 40 and the old National Road. I drove down that stretch for half an hour until I got to a place in a small town where a large truck was trying to make a turn onto a narrow street, but had to keep going back and forth and in the process held up the traffic on the highway. I tried to find routes that went around the intersection, but there were none. I ended up going five miles back on the 40 and taking the Interstate. Once I passed the point of the jam and exited back onto the 40, nearly twenty minutes had passed. Apparently the truck had just let the motorists pass and now there was a long line of slow moving vehicles on the 40 and in front of me on the exit there were quite a few trucks that, with the heavy traffic on the highway they were heading to, were taking forever to make their turns.

One interesting thing about that section of the National Road was that it contained replicas of the old mile markers and also some of the 200 year old stone bridges were still intact (though not all of them were still used to carry traffic). Soon I crossed the state line and was back to West Virginia. Though I was at a completely different corner of the state from Green Bank, and though I had only spent four days over there, it felt like I was going back home. This stretch through the Northern Panhandle only lasted for thirteen miles, before I got into the big town of Wheeling with its old Victorian houses and its multitude of bridges crossing the Ohio River, one of which I soon crossed into Ohio.

I was debating whether to stay on the National Road in Ohio or whether to take a more scenic drive along the river. Partly because the rains started and the drivers turned on their bright lights, I opted for the river route. That route had two lanes on each side so I could distance myself from oncoming headlights like I did on a freeway. It started off fine, but soon the road narrowed to only one lane and I was stung by the oncoming headlights. As such, I turned west onto a state highway with less traffic.

This highway turned out slow and boring, so I checked my Readers' Digest book on scenic drives to see if there were any near me. I saw that Route 26 was an extension of a scenic drive they had for the hills of Southeastern Ohio and I turned onto that road. It did not end up being quite as scenic as it appeared, unfortunately, and was very slow. In fact, after I had stopped to rest somewhere, a local glanced at me and asked me if I needed help. I told him I didn't. Then he asked me where I was headed to, and I told him Cincinnati. He told me I was heading down the wrong road. Well, maybe this was not a major route to Cincinnati, but from the point where I was at this was the main road to Cincinnati.

I was back onto the faster routes an hour later. There were no direct interstates to Cincinnati from that place, so I started taking scenic highway 550. However, as soon as I got onto it, the rain began falling hard and the oncoming lights blinded me, so I made a u-turn and ended up taking the less scenic but wider U.S. 50. I took that road to Athens, where Ohio University is located and where I decided to stop for dinner.

I stopped in the historic uptown and walked around looking for a place to eat. The rain was still falling. I entered a trendy Latin restaurant, but they were busy. Then I found a dive bar that, while it attracted a cell phone heavy college crowd, did not have too many people at that hour and appeared to have good food. I placed an order for buffalo wings, but my order was taking forever and before I got my food the place started filling up and there was now no seat for me to move to away from the cell phones. As such, I canceled my order and asked for a refund. I now went to look for another place to eat. I found a fast food diner in the lower part of Athens. It still had a good amount of people, but a bit less than at the dive bar, and since it was away from the college, the people were not on their phones as much. Now after dinner I had a two and a half hour drive to Cincinnati. I got to my hotel there just after 10.

VII. The South

I headed out the drizzly morning of the following day through the Cincinnati suburbs where I had spent the night. Again I passed through downtown, this time on the freeway, and soon was across the river in Kentucky. I was headed to Nashville for the night. I soon got to the exit for the Ark Encounter, the full size replica of Noah's Ark in the hills of Kentucky. I got off the freeway debating on whether I wanted to visit it. I thought of at the most seeing it from the outside. However, once I got to the parking, I saw it cost ten dollars to park and there was no view of the ark from that point. I had a lot to see that day so I decided to skip it.

I drove down to Lexington and started a scenic drive from my Reader's Digest book. I stopped for lunch at a barbecue place in a suburban shopping center. Now that I was in the South, I wanted real Southern barbecue. I stepped into this restaurant, but it was right during lunchtime and there was a long line of people on their phones ordering at the counter. As such, I continued on. I passed through the bluegrass country right outside of the city. This was home to the thoroughbred horse ranches, some of which were quite exquisite. It is said the horses from there are so strong because of the limestone rich soil that gets into the grass that they eat. This limestone right beneath the soil was present at every highway cut and at some river cuts, including the spectacular gorge of the Kentucky River that I drove through right as I heard that the House decided to open the impeachment inquiry against Trump.

Soon I got to Pleasant Hill, the site of an old Shaker village. Having considered moving to an intentional community, this place was of interest to me, even if this community no longer existed and was now a museum with a couple shops. My only misgiving was that it had gotten unusually cold. I started my day with temperature in the 50s, but by 1 PM it had rapidly gone down to 40, the coldest I had had on this trip except for some mornings in West Virginia. Though I only had a light jacket on me, I got out of the car.

I did not walk around the grounds much, but I did enter the stores and got some bourbon filled chocolates. Then I went to their restaurant, located in an old dormitory where guest rooms were still available. The restaurant did not have too many people, so I ate there even though it was a bit pricey. They had fried chicken on the menu and I decided that since I was there I would get real Kentucky fried chicken. The chicken was very good, and later on when I passed a KFC I asked myself how could people in Kentucky eat that bad fast food version of it.

Judging by the workers at the restaurant, Kentucky appeared to be a place with very nice people. I was thinking that maybe I should move there instead of West Virginia, but I was turned off by the Southern conservatism. I talked to my waitress about other places I was planning on visiting, namely Mammoth Caves. She told me she had never been there, but we joked about how it might be a good place to visit on Halloween. Full disclosure- it was Halloween that day.

My drive that day was beautiful- much more than that highway in Ohio I had been on the previous day. While I tried not to make too many stops due to the cold, there were some places I could not resist to see. One was the site of Lincoln's boyhood home. I stopped there for a couple minutes before running back into my car. Twenty minutes down the road was the cabin where Lincoln was born. I stopped there, this time having to stop for a bit longer because I wanted to go into the Greek revival structure up the hill which housed- supposedly- the very cabin in which Lincoln was born. I went inside to view the cabin, even though more recent evidence reveals this was not the original cabin- it was built more than thirty years after Lincoln was born. Nevertheless, this was the correct area in which he was born.

I still decided to go to Mammoth Cave on Halloween, even though it was late in the day and I was not sure what would still be open when I got there at 4:30. Indeed, I saw many cars exiting on the park road, but almost no one driving in. I parked by the visitor center and went to look around. It was closed, but I found a map of the park. The main entrance to the cave was apparently only a few hundred feet away from me, and down the trail that ran through the gulch directly below me. Had the weather been warmer, I would have probably explored it, but with the temperature now at 36 I could not let myself do it. Instead, I walked into the gift shop, which was open. I found a thick jacket there and I got it from a salesman wearing a Halloween mask, even though it was a bit pricey. Then I felt better and decided to explore more of the park. I did not go to the main entrance. Rather, I found a few other entrances that were right off the main road. I drove to them, but they were sealed. Apparent you can only walk through these entrances with a guided tour and there were no tours remaining that day.

I continued on to Nashville, trying not to make it there too late. I got to my hotel right before 7 PM, a fair time compared to the 10 PM that I arrived at my place the previous night, but maybe not that early since I also went one time zone back and it was still 8 PM Eastern Time. I got to my hotel in Opryland, and was surprised at how ornate it was for the price. However, parking was expensive- you could only park valet and it cost 32 dollars for the night. As such, I parked at a lot farther away, one I was not sure I was even allowed to park in. I walked to the hotel and went to the registration, but when I gave them my name they did not find my reservation. They asked me if I was sure I made the reservation and I told them I was sure. It took them about ten minutes, but they ultimately realized my reservation was not for the Opryland Hotel, but for the slightly less fancy Inn at Opryland, their sister property which I was told many people mixed up with that hotel. I headed over to the Inn at Opryland. Not as elegant as the other place, but still comfortable and with no parking charge.

Part of my inspiration for coming to Nashville was Ken Burns's 16 hour long Country Music documentary which had just aired on PBS. Granted I was never a major country music fan, except for when it came to the really good singers like Johnny Cash and the country pop music of people like Kenny Rogers and Shania Twain. Nevertheless I did find that music interesting and an integral part of American culture and I did want to go to the city most associated with it. I was trying to find some good country stations on the radio when I was there. I did not care much for newer country, but I did like much of the classic Nashville sound of the 1960s and 70s. However, as I flipped my radio dial, I could not find any worthy stations of either newer or older country. All of them seemed to play the usual rock, hip hop, and Top 40 formats heard on radio stations everywhere else in the United States. Even WSM, the classic AM station that has been broadcasting the Grand Ole Opry for nearly a century, I did not find very appealing. Once when I tuned in in the morning, they had a long interview with a rather obscure musician. Later on in the day, they played a collection of songs about drinking and things of that nature. Maybe if you are a hard core country fan you will find that station appealing, but I did not. The one good classic country station I found was a rather obscure one at AM 950. It did not have the strongest signal, but they did play a good collection of classic country from the 1960s to the 80s. Maybe the unique music of Nashville is more to be found at cell phone filled bars and entertainment venues, but I did not go to any of them.

The following morning I did my sightseeing of Nashville. I considered visiting the Grand Ole Opry auditorium. There was a whole group of elderly tourists at my hotel who were headed for that place. But as I never once had listened to the Opry I would not go and visit that auditorium that had no architectural significance. Rather, I decided to explore more of the Opryland Hotel that I accidentally went to the previous night, as that seemed more interesting. Indeed it was interesting. It was a large complex filled with multiple enclosed atria featuring gardens of different themes. There was a tropical garden, a large enclosed waterfall, and a replica of a small Southern town sitting on an "island" in the middle of one of the atria. This was a Las Vegas or Disneyland of country music. Opryland was even more of a Disneyland when it had an amusement park when first built in the 1970s.

After spending an hour touring all the gardens of that hotel, I went to Downtown Nashville. I cruised down Broadway with its old music stores and bars surrounded by new tall buildings that seemed to go up around every corner in this thriving and growing city. My mom and other people told me I should look into Nashville for moving. Maybe that place could work for me, except for the hot and humid summers which would be unbearable.

Once I passed downtown, I realized I did not find the Ryman Auditorium, the Grand Ole Opry's venue before Opryland was built and to which, since having been restored in the 1990s, it has returned to for the winter season. That place was featured heavily in Ken Burns's documentary, but since that documentary relied on pictures of the auditorium from the 1960s and 70s, I did not recognize the place now and it took a couple tries until I finally found it. It was no longer surrounded by large parking lots- new buildings had gone up over them, and the auditorium was dwarfed by a 34 story apartment building being built right across the street. That place was more interesting for me than the newer auditorium that was less the soul of the Opry. I thought of going in for a visit, but once again I am not a huge country fan and I had other things to do that day, so I was satisfied with just seeing that place from the outside.

There is an interesting story of how the Grand Ole Opry got its name. In the 1920s, radio stations liked to play selections from "grand operas" of the likes of Puccini and Bizet. Following WSM's grand opera program, they had one of local hillbilly music that originally did not have a name. Then one day in 1927, the announcer said they would have a two hour program of grand old opera followed by one not of that music but of how a country person might pronounce that phrase- grand ole opry.

Before going to Nashville, there were two cuisines I told myself I needed to have over there- good Southern barbecue and Kurdish food. The first one of these I was looking for the previous night. I found a couple places in my guidebook, but it being an old one all the places I looked for had either gone out of business or not open when I went there. I ended up going to an Asian run seafood place instead. I would be in the South for a couple more days, so the barbecue chicken could wait. I was also not too crazy about ordering chicken at restaurants. Unless it is at a health conscious place, chicken often has a lot of antibiotics. In the morning, I went to a Kurdish place.

My mother's family is originally from Kurdish Iraq, having moved to Israel when she was six. It is very common for my parents' generation of Israelis born before the founding of that country to have been born elsewhere. With both my parents being born in different countries, having been brought to Israel as young children, and then coming to the United States, I consider myself a child of double immigrants.

My mother still likes to make Kurdish dishes, so I am highly familiar with that food. There are no Kurdish restaurants in the Los Angeles area- there used to be one but now it's closed, but Nashville has a good amount of them. It is home to the greatest concentration of Kurds in the United States.

Kurdistan was the West Virginia of the Jewish diaspora. It was a poor backwater place whose people had a reputation for being uneducated- at least that was the view of the European elite in Israel. However, its people are also very warm and friendly. And if one takes a close look at Kurds or West Virginians, one sees they are far from stupid.

I found this good Kurdish restaurant on the Nolansville Pike. I went in there right after they opened at 11 AM, having not had breakfast before. I was the only customer at the restaurant at that time besides one other, who was on his phone so I moved to the other side of the restaurant. The menu did not consist of the stews my mother likes to make, and was arguably more standard Middle Eastern than traditional Kurdish, but it was nevertheless foods Kurds commonly eat. I ordered some kabob and rice, which was very good.

When I was done eating, I told my waiter that my mother is from Kurdistan also, and he was impressed. I asked him if he was from the same town where my mother was from, He was not, but the person on his phone did happen to be from that town. He asked me if I knew any Kurdish, and I told him I did not. Being from a Jewish community, my mother and her family did not speak Kurdish, but a dialect of Aramaic that was also spoken in that region and which my uncle spent his life trying to preserve. I asked the waiter if he happened to hear of my uncle, who was quite well known among some Kurds, but he did not. He told me his story. He had come to the United States four years prior, settled in Colorado, but when he heard of the large Kurdish community in Nashville he moved there. I asked him if he liked living in Nashville and he told me he did, despite the summer heat.

After the Kurdish place, I was trying to think of what else there was to see in Nashville. I decided I had seen all I wanted and was now ready to head to

Memphis- my next overnight stop. I took the surface streets out of the city. Once I passed Vanderrbilt University, there was one more landmark I wanted to see- the Acropolis. Nashville was once known as the Athens of the South, both because of its large population of intellectuals and its Acropolis replica, but by the 1960s "Music City USA" became its official and much more well known motto, much to the dislike of the city's traditional aristocracy.

I had been to the original Athens before, but the day I was there there was a national strike so I could not get to the Acropolis. Now was my chance to see its replica in Nashville. I went inside. This structure was built to look like the one in Athens looked before it fell into ruins, and in the replica's interior there was a large painted statue of the goddess Athena. It also had a basement with art galleries, but that did not interest me as much, except for the exhibit on the World's Fair that was held in Nashville in 1921 and for which the Acropolis was built.

After the Acropolis, I was ready to head out of Nashville. I continued down the old pikes, and was happy when I passed the suburbs and the long traffic light waits of the Friday afternoon traffic. I was not too far from the start of the Natchez Trace Parkway. In fact, Highway 100 on which I was driving on intersected with its start. In part because it headed less in the direction of the setting sun that I would soon encounter, I decided to take the Natchez Trace part of the way to Memphis.

The Natchez Trace was a project begun in by the National Park Service in the 1930s and not completed until 2005 and that established a new scenic highway following the course of an old Indian trail that was heavily traveled on in the early 1800s before steamboats using the rivers made that road obsolete. The modern parkway is essentially a primitive freeway. There are no houses or businesses along it and no direct intersections with the highways (small roads leads off the parkway to connect with the highways). However, it is only one lane in each direction, the speed limit does not exceed 50 miles per hour, commercial vehicles are prohibited from using that road, and there are numerous recreational stops along it- both historic and scenic ones.

It was while driving down this road that I heard some frightening news on the radio. Throughout my trip, my mother kept asking me when would I return, not wanting me to continue spending a lot of money on hotels. While I was planning on being back within six days, I also did not really want to return to that Southern California environment that was not good for me. Now the news on the radio confirmed this. The Maria Fire was spreading in California and the communities of Camarillo, Somis, Santa Paula, and East Ventura were all under fire watch. I was horrified. These places were all ten miles from where I lived. I had gone through two major fires in Ventura County over the past two years. While my residence was in no danger of burning, and was not in danger of burning now, there was a lot of unhealthful smoke in my area. I did not want to get back until the smoke would clear. If that would happen within a week, which would be the case if this would not be an especially large fire, I would return. But otherwise, I would take more time on my trip. I was enjoying the clean air of the forests of Tennessee and did not want to be anywhere else at the moment.

I did not make too many stops along the Trace, but I did stop at Meriwether Lewis's gravesite. Here is the story for those who do not know it. After Lewis returned from exploring the passage to Oregon with William Clark and Sacagawea, he was appointed governor of the Lousiana Territory. Though it was a prestigious job, he did not like being stuck in a desk in St. Louis- he wanted to explore places. Then in 1809 he was appointed to a government desk job in Washington DC, a more civilized place that he hated even more. Obediently he headed there, taking a boat down the Mississippi. While on the boat, he started feeling sick, and knowing where he was headed to he tried twice to kill himself and even asked the captain to do it for him. When the ship got to the fort where Memphis would later be built, he was too ill to continue traveling by boat and had to take a land route. He headed east from the fort and then turned north on the Natchez Trace. On October 10th 1809, he stopped at a tavern called the Grinder to rest. That evening, a gunshot was heard and then Meriwether Lewis was found dead. Was it a murder or a suicide?

The National Park Service's position is that it was a suicide. However, in James Michener's novel *Texas*, which I had read a few years back, he seems to lean toward it being a murder, something others have theorized also. I am inclined to side with the National Park Service. No motive was ever found for a murder, but Lewis did try killing himself before, so the most logical explanation is that he finally succeeded in doing that. I never liked it when people assumed the more negative side in things. Many people unfortunately do not see the good in humanity and when something for which they do not know the answer appears to them they assume the possibility that is the most cruel and disturbing, even if it is not the most logical one.

I went over to the pillar marking Meriwether Lewis's gravesite. I very much identified with that person. Like me, he had traveled across the United States. At age 35, only two years younger than me, he was being forced to move back to a place he did not like, a city where he would be stuck in and whose society he did not like. I was traveling down the exact same road he was traveling on to get to the type of place he did not like. When he saw that his life was doomed, he killed himself. I very much hoped I would never be compelled to take that course of action.

I continued on down the Natchez Trace. I was soon at the junction of U.S. 64 which headed straight to Memphis. It was less than two hours till sunset now, but I thought the road would not head straight in the direction of the setting sun. It indeed did not always head in that direction but depending on what course it took with its turns sometimes it went right into the setting sun. I stopped in the town of Murphysboro in front of a Mexican restaurant. I thought of just sitting there for an hour and a half until the sun would set, but even with a book to read that would be boring. I looked at my atlas and saw that the junction with highway 13 was just down the road. I would take that south back to the Natchez Trace, head into Alabama, and then take U.S. 72 into Memphis hopefully after sunset.

That was what I did. I turned onto highway 13 heading through downtown Murphysboro and stopped there for lunch. Since I had had a big breakfast with my kabobs, I only got a pie at the restaurant. I heard that the pies in these small town Southern restaurants tend to be very good. My overly sweet pie was a dentist's nightmare, but it was nevertheless very good. I then continued on my way, with less than an hour remaining until sunset. The sun was setting in my eyes on the Natchez Trace also, but since that road went south by southwest without too many turns, the sun was never directly in my eyes like it would have been on the highways heading due west.

I soon crossed into Alabama, which I found to be a very random place going to on this trip. I had been to Alabama once before, on a trip to New Orleans when I spent two nights in Mobile, though that was at the completely opposite end of the state from where I was now. There was not much to see in that corner- it was all basically farmland- but was nevertheless scenic. The harshest part of that drive was ten minutes before sunset when the road turned right in the direction of the setting sun when going over a bridge of a lake of the Tennessee River. I held up my magazine to the road, went no more than 30 even though the speed limit was 50, and made sure I had no cars in front of me. Soon the sun went behind the hill in front of me and I was able to lift my magazine and look around at the scenery. I had made it to U.S. 72 right after sunset and now took that road through Mississippi and into Memphis.

Since this was the weekend and a cheaper part of the country, I went back to my tradition of the tallest hotel in the city and on the highest floor for Memphis and my following night's stay in Little Rock. For Memphis, that was the 27 story Hilton along the city's beltline. Finding the hotel was easy, as is the case with all tall buildings that can be seen from a distance, especially if they are right by the freeway. However, getting to it was a different story. The exit was to a highway with limited turns- actually the very U.S. 72 I was traveling on but from which I transferred to a freeway right outside of the city. It took a couple tries, including driving into the parking lot of the nearby Marriott for an attempted shortcut, but I finally found my hotel's entrance after ten minutes. I checked myself into my hotel, getting a room on the 23rd floor, and now I was ready to get some good Memphis barbecue for dinner.

The computers in the lobby were out of service and I would never bring a laptop with me, so I had to find a barbecue joint the old fashioned way. I asked the person who checked me in about going to the famous Beale Street, but he would not recommend it, saying it gets jam packed on Friday nights. I looked in my restaurant guide for some good barbecue places, hoping they would still be in business. I found one a few miles from my hotel and headed there. They were still in business, but they closed their dining room at the unusually early hour of 9 PM and I got there only two minutes before nine, so I had to order my food to go (even though there was still a crowd at the restaurant).

I drove the fifteen minutes back to the Hilton. When I got up to my room, I realized I forgot my key so I had to go back to my car to get it. When I got back to my room, I realized I needed to get a drink, so I went to the vending machines on my floor. They did not have any soft drinks- only water, but there was a sign saying soft drinks were found on alternating floors. I went up to the 24th floor, but there were no soft drinks there either. Soft drink vending machines used to be ubiquitous in hotels, but in these more health conscious days they are disappearing. Personally I am not a fan of this trend, as there are still many people- including myself- who will not drink water. I now had to go to the lobby floor and get a juice at the coffee counter. In front of me there was a person taking a long time getting a smoothie, so not wanting my food to get cold, I got my drink right after the person ordered his smoothie but before it was made, saying that I was in a bit of a hurry. The counter lady was very nice and said she was very happy I was there. Now, nearly half an hour after I got my food, I was finally ready to eat. The barbecue chicken with the hot sauce was amazing, and indeed some of the best barbecue I ever tasted. I found it weird to be eating it in a room of the Hilton, though.

One thing I liked about Memphis was that the people there were very nice, especially the African American food servers at my hotel. The server at my breakfast table also told me she was happy I was there. I got into a long conversation with her about my road trip, and she was amazed I had driven all the way across the country. I showed her some of my pictures, including some artsy pictures I had just taken of the hotel's architecture. I could not talk to her for too long, however. I had a 10:30 appointment for a tour of Graceland.

Memphis was more of my music scene than Nashville. This was a city built on blues, rock 'n' roll, and, perhaps more importantly, Elvis. I had long wanted to visit Graceland, and now I was there.

We had a good introductory video at the visitor center on Elvis's career, but when we boarded the bus for the short drive across the street to the actual mansion, it was not good for my electrosensitivity. We were all given iPads with videos on the mansion. I am not sure if the videos streamed from the Internet- I managed to put my device on airplane mode and the app still worked. However, being in a bus filled with people using their devices did give me a bad headache that stayed with me for much of the day.

Nevertheless, Graceland was interesting. I kept a distance from my tour group, watching the presentations on my iPad but on airplane mode. The house looked very 70s, and one of the houses with better 70s décor. It reminded me quite a lot of the house from the latest Annabelle movie that was set in that decade. It also reminded me of the house of a girl I liked in high school whose décor was dated but well styled, and which at one time appeared in Sunset Magazine. Because that house was quite well known locally at one time I actually called it the "Mar Vista Hill Graceland" without yet having visited the original Graceland to see the similarities.

After Graceland, I tried going to Beale Street, but when I got there it was jam packed. Usually it does not get too busy there during the day, even on weekends, but that day there was a sports show broadcasting from there so it was way more busy than usual. So now I went to the Civil Rights Museum at the site of the Lorraine Motel where Martin Luther King was killed. I tried to get into the museum, but it too was crowded. Rather, I went to an extension of the museum across the street. That was the building housing the boarding house from which James Earl Ray allegedly shot King. There was a whole exhibit there about the events leading up to the incident.

Personally, I have a hard time believing James Earl Ray was the one who did it. Yes, Ray was a career criminal. Yes, he did stay at the part of the boarding house from where the gunshots came. Yes, he pled guilty to doing it. However, neither was there a clear motive for him to do it. Ray was an opportunist who wanted easy money, he was not a person with strong enough racist views to make him want to assassinate Martin Luther King. It appears more likely to me that it was done by the police and/or government agents and that Ray, because he already had a strong criminal background, was cast as a scapegoat and pressured, under threat of the death penalty if he did not, to plead guilty to the assassination.

At the end of my tour, I asked the black woman working at the gift shop if she thought it was Ray who did it or if it was a conspiracy. She said that she did not know the answer, but personally she also thought it was the FBI or people from the government. I do not think it was the FBI, at least not primarily. The FBI most wanted to discredit King, not to kill him. I do not believe the FBI would be that evil to want to kill Martin Luther King, and also they had many intelligent people who knew that if he were to be killed he would become a martyr and not the best way to invalidate King. More likely it was the Memphis Police, and /or a local, state, and/or federal government agents among whom there were people willing to kill Martin Luther King, and there is plenty of evidence (though inconclusive) linking some of these agencies to the assassination. I also find credible the theory that Ray did it for his brother or another agent in exchange for money. The theory that it was the mafia I don't buy too much either. Once again, what would have been their motive?

After the assassination exhibit, I went back to the main part of the museum, which was now a bit less crowded. That museum chronicled the history of civil rights and discrimination in the United States from the time of the first European settlers up to the 1960s. I went through the museum quite fast, as I already knew much of this history. The one interesting thing in that museum was the room where Martin Luther King stayed before his assassination. That room was restored to its 1968 appearance, and I cut in front of a large crowd of people on their cell phones to see it.

Now I was ready to go back to Beale Street. It was now nearly 4 PM and the radio show was no longer broadcasting, so the street was no longer as busy. I went into a restaurant at the foot of Beale to have my lunch, a place that did not have too many people that time of day, and ordered a plate of fried catfish. After lunch, I got back out on Beale to explore some more. Now it was actually empty. The street was still blocked off to motorists, so with the whole width of the street being pedestrian only it felt nearly deserted. Still, I was not too crazy about Beale Street other than it being a landmark. Even with not a lot of people, there were still a lot of smokers.

I still had more than an hour left until sunset at that point, and that meant more time to explore Memphis before I could hit the road again. I went to the city's pyramid. Because Memphis, Tennessee was named after the ancient city in Egypt, it was decided it too should have a pyramid. The one in Tennessee is a modern black glass coated pyramid that looks like a clone of the Luxor in Las Vegas. When I walked into the pyramid, I was surprised to find that this fancy 320 foot tall structure was almost exclusively dedicated to... a Bass Pro Shop.

It was not always that way. It was originally built as a sports stadium, but it was not quite up to pro standards and when new stadiums were built the teams moved out of the pyramid. In 2015, after sitting abandoned for some time, Bass Pro moved in, and put in a truly one of a kind store. The store occupies the entire first floor of the building, and except for a couple of mezzanines and an observation deck at the top, the whole structure is open to the ceiling. Within the store are a bowling alley, a restaurant, an aquarium, and what I found the most interesting- artificial lakes with plastic swamp trees coming out of them. It looked like some of the recreations at Disneyland of certain areas that lay not too far from Memphis. There were many people trying to get into the elevator for the observation deck, so I skipped that. Rather, I visited a boutique hotel that had just opened on one of the mezzanines.

After the pyramid, I was trying to think of what else there was to see in Memphis. There was no reason for me to be in there until sunset, but then I realized there was one more place worth visiting in town- the Sun Studio where Elvis cut his first records.

I now headed east to that building. It was a bit difficult to get to with the way some of the roads are laid out, but I managed to get there before they closed for the day. I walked into the old brick building, and found myself in a 50s style café. I asked the person at the counter if that was where Elvis had cut his first record and I was told it was. Then I asked if there were any tours or exhibits there, and I was told the 5:30 tour, the last one of the day, had just left a few minutes prior but that I could go up the stairs and catch up with them. That was what I did now.

The upstairs portion had a few exhibits, but the downstairs portion behind the café was the real interesting part. That is where the studio was. The building had housed the Union Hotel, and when that property was renovated in 1953 it was decided to add a recording studio to it. A year after, rock 'n' roll became popular and Sam Philips discovered talents such as Elvis and Johnny Cash whom he brought to record there. Improvements in recording meant that the studio had become obsolete by 1959 and thus relocated down the street. The new studio is a private facility not open to tours. As for the old studio, it reopened in the 1980s after Tom Petty and other rock stars rediscovered it, considering the place hallowed ground. The new one currently functions as an active recording studio when tours are not present.

That place certainly has a lot of history. However, it is not the place where rock 'n' roll was born. Black musicians had been making upbeat rhythm and blues records for at least a decade before it became known as rock 'n' roll. That music's fusion with country and other influences was only a natural progression once whites began listening to and emulating black music and blacks began listening to and emulating white music. The introduction of electric guitars was also a natural progression once improved technology allowed them to be manufactured for less money. Rock 'n' roll was not something invented by someone at a studio.

At the end of the tour, I asked my tour guide, who was white, if he thought Memphis was a good place to live and he told me he did, and that he had lived there his whole life. Then I asked him if he found the people to be nice there and he told me he did. Then I asked him if there was a lot of racism there. He hesitated with the answer but then told me "Of course you will find some racism here. This is after all the place where Martin Luther King was killed." Then I asked him "Do you think it was James Earl Ray who did it or do you think it was people from the government?" He told me "There is the conspiracy theory, but I don't believe in those things." I find it interesting when some groups of people believe in one narrative and another group believes in a completely different narrative, even when that narrative is contradictory to what the "experts" tell us. It makes it very difficult to know what the truth is and who to believe.

Memphis does have some nice people, amazing barbecue, and iconic tourist attractions. However, I was not too impressed with the city. It has a lot of poverty- there is a reason why Memphis became home of the blues. It also does not have a lot of diversity. Almost all the people there are either black, i.e. descendents of African slaves in this country, or white, i.e. descendents of Europeans who have been in this country for multiple generations. This contrasts with Nashville, with its thriving economy that brings in a growing population and a diversity of new immigrants from Africa, Kurdistan, Mexico, and other places. Even the tourist attractions in Memphis are nice to see once in your life, but they are not places I would return to unless I were to take other people to visit them. It is not a city like San Francisco or New York that you want to keep coming back to, though I am sure I will be back there someday on a future road trip of mine.

I left Sun Studios right at sunset and was now able to start my two hour drive west to Little Rock. I crossed the wide Mississippi in the twilight sky and soon was in another new state- Arkansas. Little Rock comes at you without warning. Because the city has only 200 000 people and very little in the name of suburbs, one minute you drive down a dark highway and a few minutes later you cross the Arkansas River and are right in Downtown Little Rock. I did not know exactly where to exit for my hotel, so I got off near Bill Clinton Drive and looked for the 19 story Marriott on the skyline.

The hotel was right in downtown, and since parking at the hotel was a bit expensive I parked at a lot a couple blocks away. The hotel had some interesting 1980s architecture with its use of red brick and glass, as well as an atrium that around the elevators went all the way to the top of the building. The person who checked me in had a local accent and I have to say looked a bit like Bill Clinton. Now I was ready to take the elevator up to the 18th floor, where I was upgraded to a river view room.

After checking in, I walked down the street looking for a place to eat. I found a sushi bar. Not having to eat Southern food all the time and somewhat missing the food I had in California, I went in there. I noticed throughout my travels that even though it is a Japanese food item, different regions of the United States have unique varieties of sushi, some of which are almost never seen outside the region. There is, for example, an Oregon Roll. At this restaurant, I got the Arkansas River Roll.

The following morning, I has a beautiful view of the river as the sun was coming up and hitting the bridges. At first, the river was enveloped in fog, but that soon cleared. When I left my hotel, I tried going to the Clinton Library, but that was closed for a special event and would not open until 1 PM- too late if I wanted to get to Dallas in time. Instead, I headed to the place where he served as governor- the Arkansas State House.

I was going to visit the places where Bill Clinton spent different parts of his life in reverse chronological order. I was already at the White House once in the

1990s when he was president. Now I was going to the place where he served right before that. Later that day, I would go to Hot Springs where he went to high school, and then to Hope where he was born. I came of age during Clinton's presidency, and despite his occasional sexual improprieties and his administration's tough on crime policies (which I was opposed to even in the 1990s), I thought he was a fairly good president. He had good economic and foreign policies, and he did not get us into long unnecessary wars like Bush nor was he the bully that Trump was. The only other president in my lifetime who might have been better than Clinton was Obama, but he was not without flaws either.

I got to the State House right before 10 AM. I did not think I could get inside as it was a Sunday, so I just walked around the outside of the building. Soon a guard spotted me and I asked him if the building was open. He told me it would open at 10. I waited a couple minutes for the doors to be unlocked and then walked in. I had been to several state capitol buildings on previous trips. They are almost always grand buildings, but they also all look the same. Nearly all of them are replicas of the U.S. Capitol, and Arkansas's was no exception.

The main thing I wanted to see in Little Rock was Central High School, and I went there right after the Capitol. This was the place where the major Civil Rights battle over the integration of public schools was fought. In the 1950s, Central was considered one of the best high schools in the Mid-South. It had a wide variety of programs and a grand brick building to show for it. However, blacks were not allowed to attend that school. Then in 1957 Little Rock decided it would begin integrating its schools by allowing nine blacks to attend Central. Many white parents and students were opposed to this, and Governor Faubus sided with them. After the "Little Rock Nine" had their first few days at school, they were told they could no longer go to school there and the governor brought in the state's National Guards to enforce that ruling. As that incident attracted national news and the country saw how racist Arkansas could be, President Eisenhower met with Faubus asking him to let the blacks go to school there and reminding him that the Supreme Court decided that public schools needed to be integrated. Finally the governor relented, and now the National Guards had to be called in not to bar the Little Rock Nine from entering the school but to escort them in against a racist white mob.

The school is still functioning, but since 1998 it has been part of the National Park Service. I found this arrangement very interesting for a school and I had a lot of questions as I entered the visitor center, which was located across the street. I asked the person at the front desk if the school was really owned by the

National Park Service and he told me it was, and that this was the only such public school in the country to have that arrangement. Then I asked him if a lot of people visited that site and I was told they had 1300 the previous day.

It was empty when I walked in, but soon the museum began filling up. The crowd was quite varied, including both families with children and old couples. As I was reading the displays, I told an older couple who were standing next to me that it is so disturbing the people at the school were so aggressively opposed to the new students coming in just because they were black. The guy responded by saying it was a different time. I told him it was not that different of a time and that we still have a lot of racism now. It is just expressed in slightly different ways.

After the museum, I went to see the school. While tours are sometimes offered, none were being offered that day because school was in session, even though it was the weekend. I still, however, could see the place from the outside. It truly was a beautiful campus with an impressive main building that looked like one at a university. I imagined myself being a high schooler who was not wanted at that school because of the color of my skin or other traits, something that was not difficult for me to imagine given my life experiences.

The thing that bothered me about the Civil Rights museums of the South, at least the two that I visited, was that they oversimplified the struggles. They portrayed Civil Rights as almost exclusively between black and white, with very little mention of other disenfranchised groups, and as something that was largely done by the 1960s. This history was then romanticized through old cars parked outside the Lorraine Motel and a restored 1950s gas station across the street from Little Rock Central High. No, the civil rights struggle did not end in the 1960s. Anyone who has an open mind can see that we still have major struggles with racism to this day- police brutality more commonly occurring against blacks, an achievement gap still found in "integrated" schools that are not fully integrated, sexual harassment of women, and a bunch of other things.

I may be a college educated white man with money to travel, but the Little Rock Nine was my story. Because I have Asperger's, I was regularly denied going to good schools. I was often placed in special education, where I was in a segregated environment for people with disabilities, and often in one geared for lower functioning students even though I had a superior IQ. When I was allowed to attend non-special education schools, I was placed in sub-par ones where I was regularly bullied by the students and treated cruelly by the staff, an experience not too different from the Little Rock Nine. And one school that I really wanted to attend but was denied had a main building that looked just like the one of Little Rock Central.

Now I was off to Hot Springs. Though this is a National Park, it is different from nearly all the others in that it is not completely natural. In addition to the mineral springs and the forested hills surrounding them, it also preserves the ornate century old bathhouses that used to be popular with vacationers. Ever since I first saw pictures of the canyon lined at its bottom with tall whitewashed brick hotels I knew I wanted to visit there.

I took the back scenic road that led me right into the northern part of the town of Hot Springs and to the start of the canyon known as Bathhouse Row. This was definitely an interesting place. It had some thriving boutiques, some of them upscale, but many of the old tall buildings seemed abandoned. I had a lot of questions for the people in town. I found out most of these buildings really were abandoned, at least in the floors above the ground level, and that only one of the tall historic hotels was still functioning.

I walked into the still functioning hotel. It was truly ornate on the inside. Another thing I was wondering about Hot Springs was its history of mob activity. On an episode of his 1990s cult classic TV Nation, Michael Moore chided Bill Clinton for bragging about being from the quaint town called Hope when he really was just born there and spent his formative years in Hot Springs, a town that Moore described as being one of the centers for mob activity at that time. I was wondering if the mob part was really true. I am not too inclined to believe Michael Moore. Despite his comic façade, he can be a harsh person who exaggerates things in a very negative way. When I asked the person at the hotel, he told me he did not know too much about that part of the town's history, but he did say that because it was a National Park the mob would not want to do their business there. They would not want to do it in a federal territory where there were likely to be government agents. Someone else told me that Hot Springs was considered neutral ground for the mob. From what I ended up gathering, there was some mob activity in Hot Springs that included them operating some hotels, but it was not any more intense than in many other parts of the country.

I continued walking through the town's historic center, walking on the promenade up the hill from Bathhouse Row and which bordered on the unbuilt hills owned by the National Park Service. The whole scene felt like an Italian village with the hills and the ornate stuccoed spa buildings below. There were public faucets in the park for the spring water. I touched some of this water and it was scalding hot. In the spa treatment facilities, that water is either mixed with colder water or allowed to cool down. I walked to the end of the promenade and returned on Bathhouse Row, where I walked into the old spa buildings that were open. Only one of them still offered spa treatments, besides the one that I mentioned earlier. The rest of the spas closed between the 1960s and 80s as that treatment fell out of fashion. Two of these two and three story buildings still had boutique hotels, but no spa treatments. One historic spa building now served as the National Park Service visitor center which preserved the facilities used by the spa goers, including the changing rooms. The rest of the buildings contained shops and restaurants. Despite the demise of most of the spas, this was still a thriving town with a lot of potential. As such, it was unfortunate to see the taller buildings in town sitting abandoned. These buildings should be converted into loft apartments, or into a unique type of office or storage space. The potential for these uses exists in Hot Springs. Otherwise, they will sit abandoned to the point where they deteriorate beyond repairs. If these buildings have to be demolished due to public safety concerns, something that would not be the case if the buildings were still occupied and well maintained, that will be a tragedy. It will be a loss of the landmarks that define Hot Springs.

Before leaving the town, I sought out the observation tower at the top of the hill behind Bathhouse Row. The drive was three miles long up a slow road. I thought I was wasting my time going there, but I could not turn around either as the road was one way. I got to the tower ten minutes later. The elevator to the top would be packed so I opted for the stairs. The stairs went up the exterior of the tower and were quite steep. I went up the first few flights, thinking I would reach the top soon. This was quite intense. Normally, I am not scared of heights. However, being on the exterior of this building with the wind hitting it and only separated from the outside by a metal grate, this was quite scary. I asked some people who were walking down if there was much more to climb and they told me there was. As such, I took a couple pictures and then headed back down. Once I got to the lobby I debated whether I wanted to take the elevator. The elevator was not crowded now, so I got in. There was only one family inside with me and they did not go on their phones.

After enjoying the spectacular view from the top of the tower, I was ready to leave Hot Springs. I only had an hour left until sunset now, so while driving back down Bathhouse Row I debated stopping at one of the fine restaurants. However, I just had a large lunch three hours earlier and was still not hungry for dinner at 4:15. Plus, the road was heading south and not directly into the setting sun so I was fine. I was fine until the road swung to the west at the edge of town.

That was when I decided to stop for dinner even though it was still early. For the second night in a row, I stopped at a Japanese place.

I was not sleeping too well the past couple nights, and now on the five hours I had left to Dallas this began to show. After I got to the interstate, I had to pull off to take a nap. I rested for about fifteen minutes and it was a good nap that got me more energetic. I got back on the freeway, but did not remain on it for long. Five minutes after I got back on there was a sign saying that there was a long backup due to a crash, so I got off to take the older highway. There were several others doing the same. I stayed on U.S. 67 for a good distance after the closure, even though it was night and I could not see that much. That highway went through Hope, Bill Clinton's storied birthplace, and I was not too far from there.

I did not have a map of Hope and did not know where Clinton's birthplace was, so I tried following signs once I got into the city. I passed a sign that went too fast for me to read, so I turned back around to read it again. It merely said that the visitor center and attractions were farther down, so I was glad I did not miss the birthplace. Soon I got to Downtown Hope. I turned onto Main Street and was thinking to myself this was the Hope Bill Clinton talked about. The visitor center was closed at that hour, so I had to ask the locals. The town was quite dreary, despite having some nice historic bank buildings. It very much of the poor place Clinton described it as. It also appeared to have a large Mexican population. Arkansas was the first place I saw coming back from New York where there was a significant Mexican influence on mainstream rural and small town culture, when I saw a stand on the back road to Hot Springs selling hot tamales in addition to the standard American fare. This was a sign I was approaching the Southwest, and California. Walking into the Mexican grocery store to ask where the birthplace was made me feel, except for the cold weather, like I was back in California. The proprietor did not speak English too well and I had to repeat my question a couple times, but he finally told me to head across the railroad tracks and turn left. Those directions were rather vague. I turned left past the tracks, driving a mile parallel to the 67 until I got to the next main road. I found myself by a Little Caesar's. I went inside and asked the young Hispanic woman where the Clinton house was and she told me it was right next to me past the railroad overpass. This time, I found the house. It was not open, but I was able to walk outside and be satisfied with seeing the place where he served as President, where he served as Governor, where he grew up, and now where he was born. It was a relatively fancy house and made me question how poor he really was growing up, but then again politicians like to exaggerate things. Plus, the house was home to a large family, so he could not have been too wealthy.

After the Clinton house, I got back on the fast Interstate and told myself no more stops. I did not want to arrive in Dallas too late. I only made one quick stop in Texarkana to go to the restroom. I was driving through the Texas night counting down the miles I had to Dallas, and growing increasingly tired. I was glad when I entered the metropolitan area and when I got to the I-635 I would take to my North Dallas hotel. By then by then it was 10:20, I was very exhausted, and still had another ten miles to go. It was actually 11:20 for me, as we had just gone back to Daylight Standard Time the previous night. Ten minutes later I got to the 75 freeway and the cluster of tall buildings at its junction. I looked on the horizon for the Westin but could not find it. I exited past the tall buildings, headed back the other way on the frontage road, and now I saw my hotel. I was ready to go to my room at the end of this exhausting day, but first I had to go on their computers to check my messages. Then I checked in, went to my room on the 15th floor, and crashed into bed.

VIII. The West

I woke up at 9 the following morning, having slept for more than nine hours, most of which were productive for a change, and feeling well rested. I admired the view from my hotel of suburbs interspersed by tall buildings at random intervals. This landscape is to be found in most large U.S. cities, but in some Texas cities this mix is even more intense.

Dallas-Fort Worth was a place I was quite excited to go to, as I had a friend over there. Marie from Honeycomb in Manhattan Beach was studying at Texas Christian University and told me she would meet up with me. Our original plan was for me to drive out to Fort Worth to meet her at noon and then I would continue to my next stop of Odessa. However, she had Facebooked me the previous day realizing she had class then and would not be able to meet me until 4:50. That was a bit too late for me if I did not want to get to Odessa too late, but I had not seen any friends or family in a week, so I agreed to meet her at 4:50. That gave me the whole day to explore Dallas.

My first stop was a Pakistani restaurant for a late breakfast. I had heard of how Dallas has a large Pakistani community with some good restaurants. Being a fan of Indian and Pakistani cooking with its spices, I had long told myself that when I would go to Dallas I would go to one of these restaurants. I looked on Yelp to see where the good Pakistani places were and I found one five miles from my hotel. It was a hole in the wall and had some very un-Pakistani menu items: kabob in a bun, hamburgers, nachos! Having pure ethnic menus, especially for minor ethnic cuisines, is only found in California, the urban areas of the East Coast, and a few other enlightened cities. In other places, knowing not everyone likes the ethnic foods, local American dishes are found on the menus in addition: Omaha steaks at a Greek restaurant in that city, carved prime rib at a Chinese buffet in Kansas, and a bunch of hamburgers served at ethnic restaurants all over the United States. Even in California the menus are arguably tweaked to local tastes. At the Pakistani restaurant I go to by Manhattan Beach, for example, there are many Indian vegetarian items that would not be so widely consumed in meat and grain heavy Pakistan. I just don't notice it so much because that is where I'm from. As for me, I ordered the lamb biryani. The waitress asked me if I liked the food and I told her it was really good.

After my "lunchfast" (a lunchtime breakfast with lunch food that is the first meal of the day), I gave myself a tour of Dallas. As I was driving, I was singing to myself the theme from the classic TV series named after that city. Though it was a bit before my time, I still very much liked its opening sequence and 80s theme music. I found myself driving past the stately homes of University City en route to Southern Methodist University, where a few of my Manhattan Beach friends had gone to school. I walked around their campus and into one of their historic buildings before the cell phones got too much for me. Then I drove by the George W. Bush Library. I debated whether to go in, as it was just another museum and I was never a huge fan of W. However, this would be a good place to reminisce about the 2000s and the president and news events from when I was in college, so I went in. I felt the museum whitewashed Bush's legacy and presented him as this great person who loved his family and was for the environment (the building was LEED certified), even though in reality he often sided more with industry than with environmentalists. But then again, this was the Bush Library built and run by supporters of Bush, so of course they would show him as a good president. And in many ways, he does seem, looking back, much more quaint and a better decision maker than Trump was, at least on issues not relating to war.

The one place I most wanted to see in Dallas, and which I intended on seeing even if I was going to go to Fort Worth at noon, was the place where Kennedy was shot. That was where I headed now. I got to the eastern part of downtown, drove west down Elm Street on the road Kennedy went on in his final moments of consciousness, passing through the tall downtown buildings in a scene that no longer looked as it did in the 1963 newsreel footages. Soon I saw a brick building at the edge of downtown and knew that was the Texas Schoolbook Depository. I went past that building, onto the park area where three east west streets of downtown converge and where on the right side there is a freeway entrance. That was the spot where Kennedy was shot.

I had to go back and take some pictures of that very historic spot, so once I got to the next intersection I made a U-Turn and headed back through Dealey Plaza, as it is known, and found parking at the site of the Texas Schoolbook Depository where a museum existed on the sixth floor. The parking there cost twelve dollars. A bit expensive, but I was in a hurry to get to Fort Worth on time, so I parked there. I went out to Dealey Plaza to take pictures of the site where it happened, and standing by the grassy knoll from which a second shooter is theorized to have struck Kennedy. I was debating whether to go into the museum with its hefty price tag. I ended up going in there because that was the site from where Lee Harvey Oswald fired the fatal bullets (assuming he was the one who did it). I did not read all the panels in the museum- I did not have too much time. I was more interested in looking out of the sixth floor window at the view Oswald had. One panel that I found quite interesting and creepy was one that said Kennedy died at Parkland Hospital. I immediately thought of the town in Florida with the same name where another shooting happened 55 years later.

I have heard many different theories about who really killed Kennedy. At the end of my brief ten minute visit I asked someone at the visitor center "So do you think Lee Harvey Oswald did it?" She told me "He probably had a part." That is what I think also. Most likely, he was the one who fired the shots, but I do not believe he acted alone. Almost no political assassination is the work of only one person, it is only one person who fires the shots, at least there is only one person getting caught firing the shots. I would not deem the second shooter theory unlikely. With Martin Luther King, I am not so sure James Earl Ray did it- the evidence in that case seems a bit sketchy. However, with JFK, the evidence does support that Oswald at least had a major part in the shooting.

Now it was time to go to Fort Worth and meet Marie. Though it was still only 3:30 and I had until 4:50 for the thirty mile drive, I wanted to make it there before rush hour traffic. I also wanted to get some lunch before meeting her. I entered the freeway right at the entrance JFK's motorcade was going to take and got to Fort Worth within half an hour, having no traffic jams on the way. I proceeded to the city's legendary stockyards, which had a collection of good steak restaurants. I made my way to a large parking lot. There was a sign saying that Fort Worth is where the west begins. It sure felt that way, with the bull pens in the distance and the smell of hay and manure. I was also a bit sad, as that meant I would soon be back in California with all the problems I had there. What I could not find were the restaurants, at least not ones that were open at that time. Realizing I would not have time to eat there and make it to TCU on time, I walked around the complex a bit before getting back into my car and driving to TCU.

I got to TCU ten minutes early. Marie told me to meet her by the basketball stadium. I tried to look for any boards with campus maps, as many of these places had in the pre-smartphone era, but I could not find any. I made my way to the campus gym asking the girls at the reception if that was where the basketball stadium was. They told me they did have basketball there, and that I should call my friend to make sure she was there. The only problem was that I did not have a cell phone. I asked them if there was any other basketball place on campus, as this definitely was a gym and not a stadium. It took them a while to understand what I was asking them, but then they told me the stadium was farther down the hill. I asked them if they had a map of campus but they did not.

I walked in the direction the girls told me. I finally found the sports complex and the place where they had basketball. I looked outside and did not see Marie. I was wondering if this was the right place, or maybe she really meant the gym. I also hoped she was not standing me up like all the others who did that. I walked into the stadium's lobby, and someone was asking me "Can I help you?" I told him that I was looking for a friend. He started asking me many questions and inquiring about my visit. He did not ask me to leave, but he did make me feel unwelcome. Many Americans have this notion that because you don't go to school somewhere, you look a certain way, you talk a certain way, or because you appear older than your friends, you are likely up to no good. Because of my Asperger's, I experience this quite a lot. I walked all the way around the stadium complex, getting quite lost on the way due to the unusual locations of the access points, before getting back to the lobby at least five minutes later. I exited the building now where I first entered, and walked a bit farther down to another entrance. Now I saw a girl from the back sitting on one of the benches. I knew immediately this was Marie.

We were both so happy to see each other, and she was very excited that I drove to Texas to see her. She only had less than an hour, but she gave me a tour of the campus. I was not too bothered by students on their phones now, as it was late in the day and there were not too many students around. We walked to the famous frog statue representing the school's mascot, where we took some pictures and did the school's hand signs. Marie was telling me how proud she was of her school and that TCU was the main thing people associate with Fort Worth. I asked her what about the Stockyards. She told me that that and TCU were the two main things. I asked her if she liked living in Fort Worth and she told me she did but did not think she would stay there after college. She told me she liked the Southern hospitality there. I told her that is something I like about those places also and that it also seems like people there are more honest than in California. My one issue was that the people would be too conservative there, and she told me you definitely found that in Fort Worth. Dallas was quite a liberal place, but Fort Worth not so much.

Then Marie had to go to her meeting and I had to start driving to Odessa. I was very happy I got to see her for our brief visit. I realized there still were some nice people from Greater Los Angeles, like Marie who took time out of her busy day to meet up and did not flake out on me. We made plans to meet up over her winter break when she would be back in town. The time I spent with her in Fort Worth was a welcome break from the loneliness I had experienced on the road and I was in much better spirits after the visit.

Before hitting the highway, I went to get lunch, even though it was dinner time by now. This time I went back to the Stockyards, knowing now where the restaurants were. The Stockyards has a good collection of restaurants for meat lovers. My dad told me about the time he went to Fort Worth for business and his group went to eat there. There was a vegetarian guy from India in his group and all he could order were some potatoes and broccoli. As for me, I got the Rocky Mountain Oysters- fried bull testicles. I had that dish once before in Denver when I went to a historic restaurant that specializes in that dish. In Southern California, however, despite its wide diversity of ethnic restaurants, this dish is nowhere to be found. A friend of mine with a Youtube channel on bizarre foods told me that the closest he came to finding that dish in Southern California was getting some bull testicles at a Mexican grocery store and then preparing the dish himself. As such, I like to get that dish whenever I go to a restaurant in the non-coastal west that serves it. At the Denver restaurant, it was very good and tender. At this place in Fort Worth, not so much. In case you are wondering, Rocky Mountain Oysters taste like veal. This makes sense, as veal is also often prepared fried and breaded. Also, a veal is a young cattle. Bull testicles contain the material that develops into young cattle.

Now it was time to hit the highway. It was 7 PM and I hoped I would not get to Odessa too late. Had I known in advance Marie could only meet me at 4:50, I would have spent the night closer to Fort Worth. However, this was a last minute change and I already had my hotel reservations, so I endured having a long day's drive to my destination. I still had to stop for dinner. I am not someone who will give up on having three meals a day, whether it is in West Virginia or in Texas. I got onto the business loop of I-20 in Abilene looking for a place to eat. I was sure Abilene had some nice parts, but the whole route along that highway was run down. Finally I found a hole in the wall Mexican place. I got a quesadilla there, which was not that good, and continued on.

After I got back onto the Interstate, I was getting sleepy. There is a reason I call Interstates "hypnosis highways"- the monotony of the scenery can make one drowsy, especially when late in the day or when one is not well rested. I got off at a highway rest area, but could not nap there with the proximity to the noisy freeway and the bright overhead lights. As such, I got off at the next town, went to an empty parking lot, and rested there. I was exhausted, and when I woke up I could not believe how much time had passed- one hour. Never before had I managed to fall asleep in my car for more than a small fraction of that time. I got up feeling better rested and drove on, but with it being past midnight the "hypnosis highway" effect came back. I got back off on the business loops- old

U.S. 80- to wake myself up, including the one that went through Odessa's neighboring town of Midland. Midland is where George W. Bush grew up and I was going to go past his childhood home, but it was too late for that. I was satisfied with getting a quick glimpse of their downtown from the business loop. That business loop continues into Odessa and I stayed on it until I got to the surface highway leading to my hotel. I had a hard time finding it this time, with it not being a tall building, and I was trying to remember on what road it said to turn, which was a bit difficult when I was tired. Finally, after looking for about twenty minutes, I found the hotel. It was 1:30 in the morning and I was prepared to go straight to bed. I did not even want to check my messages, but then I decided I would send a quick e-mail to my mother so that she would not worry about me. I crashed into bed and told myself I would try to sleep as long as possible.

I only managed to sleep until 8:30 the following morning, when I went to the lobby to get my breakfast. I checked my e-mails and my mother asked me jokingly if I had arrived at the Black Sea, in reference to the other Odessa. I gave myself a quick tour of the city before getting back on the freeway. This was clearly the West. Since Dallas-Fort Worth, and especially since Arkansas where I last saw rural scenery in the daytime, the country had shifted from densely wooded forests to empty desert. I had been to the "west" many times before, but coming from coastal California, which is arguably west of this West, this always for me was the "Wild East". Now, coming from the East Coast and heading west, I really knew what was meant by going west.

The landscape on this mostly flat terrain was bleak desert dotted with sagebrush and oil wells. This was the Permian Basin, so named after the geologic period which produced the vast oil deposits of this area. I had a clearer view of this landscape once I got off the freeway heading north to Carlsbad Caverns. The road here was full of oil trucks that I was trying to go around. These trucks are very slow and the toxic fumes they emitted were noticeable. I was more than relieved when I passed the ridge marking the end of the basin and the oil fields.

Soon I had crossed into New Mexico. Driving across state boundaries, the immediate change that is most noticeable is the speed limit. Texas is very generous with its speed limits, allowing people to drive 75 miles per hour on its open two lane roads. New Mexico plays it a bit more safe. Even though the road was now four lanes, the speed limit was only 65. I personally like the higher speed limits. The average person would want to go faster than 65 on an open and divided four lane highway. Raising the speed limit to 70 or 75 does not make accidents much more serious or unavoidable. On the contrary, if drivers know they can be within the law if they drive 75, other drivers who less care about the law will not need to make dangerous passes of cars going 65 so they can drive the higher speeds they want. We should probably set speed limits somewhere between New Mexico's and Texas's. As I saw on my next road trip, Texas lowers the speed limit to a safe one when the highway passes through a town, but sometimes raises it back to 75 while there are still houses on the road.

I was headed to Carlsbad Caverns National Park. My sixth grade history teacher told us about how he went there when he was a child and of how they turned off the lights for a minute so the visitors could experience the natural pitch blackness of the cave. I had long found caves interesting, but knowing many caves turn off the lights, and not wanting to be in total darkness even for a minute, I told myself I would not be going in them. At a cave I passed in West Virginia, I asked the tour guide if they turned off the lights and when she said they did I did not go in. Carlsbad Caverns, however, was not a place I wanted to miss, it being one of the most spectacular cave system in the world. I decided that if the tours turn off the lights I would just go into the cave on my own at the entrance for solo hikers and go down as far as there was still some light. I called them ahead. I was told there are some tours that do that, and some that go into back parts of the cave that are guided by lanterns, but that you can go down the elevator from the visitor center into the main part of the cave to take a self guided walk and there the lights do not get turned off.

As I drove down the park road leading to the cave, a road that takes more than half an hour to drive each way, I was telling myself this better not be a waste. I did not want any surprises when I got there hearing that they do turn off the lights and then that I would not be able to see much from the natural entrance. I was also concerned that it would be stuffy inside the cave. I got to the visitor center, first looking at the souvenirs they had there. I got myself some cactus fruit candy, a specialty I like to get whenever I am in the Southwest and another product that is almost never sold in California. Carlsbad Caverns was another good radiofrequency quiet zone. There was no wi-fi even in the visitor center and cell phone service was quite poor. In the cave, of course, there was no cell service at all. Some electrosensitives are actually looking into moving to cave homes. I would never to that.

I again asked the rangers if they turn off the lights and they said no. Now I was ready to take the 775 foot elevator descent into the main part of the cave. In front of me was a family about to go on a lantern guided tour to one of the other parts of the cave. I would go down to the main part in the next elevator.

The cavern was spectacular, and I was very glad I went. The trails passing past formations of stalactites looked like something from a Jules Verne novel and got me immediately thinking of the dark rides at Disneyland. This indeed was the natural place where many of the Disney Imagineers got their inspiration from. I was also thinking of my sixth grade history teacher, and then I saw a visitor who looked just like that teacher. I was wondering if that was really him and was not prepared for the shock for running into him at that place he talked about when I finally made it there and after not having seem him in 25 years. It wasn't him.

I left Carlsbad right in time to make it to the next national park, Guadalupe Mountains, before the sun would be too low. I was heading southwest now across the southern border of New Mexico back into Texas, and back to the 75 miles per hour zone on a highway that again became only two lanes. My first stop at Guadalupe Mountains would be the visitor center, mostly because I really needed to go to the restroom. I got there at 3:15, a bit less than two hours before sunset and when the desert sun was starting to give me a hard time. After going to the restroom, I picked up a map of the park and headed out. Fortunately most of the park's sites were to the east of the visitor center so I did not need to worry about the sun. Guadalupe Mountains did not have too much to offer for the visitor unless one was interested in taking a long hike into the mountains. Nevertheless, there still were a couple easy stops.

I stopped by a trail that went past the ranch house of the area's pioneers and the surrounding desert. This ranch dated from the early 20th century, and coming from the east coast this ranch of the first white settlers looked new. We may in the West think of certain places as very historic, like this ranch I just walked by, but these places were established when New York and Philadelphia were already cities of more than a million people. They were established when the eastern part of the country and much of Western Europe were fully industrialized, when trains carried people to places in motorized comfort, and in the case of this ranch, when telephones, electricity, and automobiles reached much of this country. I longed for places that were more ancient. These are the places that, while they adapt to new ways, also preserve the old culture of a place and do not transform a place or a society to something completely unrecognizable with no regard to the past.

I was walking to a spring, which the signs said was 0.4 miles away, but it was not completely clear down which trail it was. I walked about that distance down one trail and when I did not see any signs of a spring I turned back. I was too tired to continue hiking, and the sun was still up, so I sat on a bench reading my magazine. I waited until the sun dipped below the mountains and then was able to continue driving. I drove down the dirt road to the highway, but when I got to the highway the sun was not yet behind the mountains at that point. I parked on the side of the road before the highway for about five minutes reading my magazine and waiting for the sun to go back down behind the mountains, and then I again continued. I made it past those mountains at the western end of the park, but when I came out on the other side the sun was still shining. Luckily the road had now turned south, but it would soon turn back west with the sun still up. Again, I stopped at a shelter on the side of the road, taking in the view from the top of a ridge and at the reddish landscape in the glow of sunset. I stayed there for about ten minutes, after which I estimated there were only about ten minutes left till sunset and I continued. I figured that once I would descend into the plain and the road would turn back west, the sun would be low enough to be behind the distant mountains. However, that proved not to be the case. As soon as I descended, the road turned right in the direction of the setting sun and the mountains on the horizon were in another direction. Again, I stopped on the side of the road for a few minutes. I was now right at the intersection of highways 54 and 62/ 180 and was taking pictures of the road signs along the desert landscape in the final light of day. I felt this was a classic American scene.

After the sun finally set behind the flat horizon, I continued on U.S. 62/ 180 to El Paso. The oncoming cars right next to me blinded me a little, but it was not as bad as the setting sun. I got into the outskirts of El Paso, which appeared as a dusty town by the border that some depictions show. I passed by a Walmart, thinking this might be the Walmart where the mass shooting the previous August had occurred. It wasn't. I was considering spending the night in downtown El Paso, as they have a couple of tall historic hotels there, including what was one of the first large Hiltons. However, all these hotels were either booked or under renovation, so I drove an hour farther down to Las Cruces.

I did not even drive into downtown El Paso. Unusually for this trip, I took the freeways bypassing the town to the north. This was because I did not want to get too close to the border. I had heard horror stories of U.S. citizens being detained by ICE when stopped at border patrol checkpoints, including the disturbing case of a Mexican American high school football player who was held up for 23 days without bail. I was also subject to increased suspicion by Border Patrol, due to my accent. That indeed was the case on my 2015 road trip when an agent asked me many questions and wanted to see my papers after he randomly stopped me and heard my accent. It wasn't until I told him that my parents are from Israel that he let me go. That incident happened to me during the Obama administration. Now with Trump's crackdowns on the undocumented, both

Stasia and I were quite worried about what could happen to me with Border Patrol. I brought my passport for extra documentation just in case.

I first went to New Mexico in 2015, visiting the major sites there. I fell in love with its unique culture and dynamic landscapes. This was one place in the west that had a good amount of ancient communities and culture, both of the Spanish and the Native Americans. The local food was quite interesting and very tasty- it was essentially Mexican food but a unique form of Mexican. There is a reason why that state is known as the Land of Enchantment. It is also supposedly a good place for electrosensitives. Arthur Firstenberg, one of the most outspoken electrosensitives, lives there. He had been to Green Bank before, but says he cannot handle that place because of all the electric cables. Though New Mexico does not have any cell phone quiet zones, the copper in the soil there helps absorb much of the dirty electricity. The people whom I met there seemed very nice for the most part, but I had some misgivings. I read that New Mexicans tend to be much more introverted than average, and I did not want a repeat of Oregon where the people were nice at first but did not want much to do with you. Also, the crime rate in New Mexico is among the highest in the United States.

I did not have any time to sightsee in New Mexico this trip. The following morning I got up at around 7:30, unable to sleep any longer, and headed to Arizona. Heading on the 10 west, I got to a point where the speed limit kept dropping. The next thing I knew I was coming to a border patrol stop. I was preparing to get out my passport, but luckily this time the agent just waved me through. I was quite tired that day and wanted to get to my hotel as soon as possible, but I still did take an alternate route to the hypnosis highway for half the drive- specifically U.S. highways 70 and 60. The "Old West Highway"- U.S. 70- took me through some beautiful mountain landscapes and colorful small towns. That highway ends in Globe, and from there I took the 60 into Phoenix. It began as a windy road descending a canyon, but soon after I dropped into the wide flat expanse of desert it became an urban freeway going through the suburbs of Phoenix. That was my destination for the night.

The suburbs of Phoenix are beautiful, but they are also a lot of the same. They constitute of row after row of housing complexes and shopping centers lined with palm trees and often painted in the reds and purples of the nearby mountains. I stopped at one of these shopping centers not far from my hotel for lunch. It was 85 degrees even in November- the hottest weather I had on this trip so far since I left Los Angeles during a heat wave and it felt a bit weird to be in the heat after the near freezing weather I had a few days prior.

I was staying at an Indian casino right outside of Chandler. Phoenix is surrounded by large reservations, and if there is one good thing about them it is that they serve as a break from the suburban sprawl. The sprawl of Chandler goes up to a certain road. South of it, it becomes all natural desert. Around Mesa, north of the 202 freeway at the Salt River reservation, the land becomes the farmland that is disappearing elsewhere in the Phoenix area. One exception is the multitude of casino resorts that appear just over the reservations' boundaries. I have mixed feelings about Native American casinos. I feel they have the potential to recast Native Americans in a bad light by having them be operators of establishments that are home to heavy drinking, smoking, and problem gambling. And if they are allowed to build humongous structures that are out of step with the natural surroundings, what does it say about their supposed environmental ways? However, who are we to say what they can or can't do on their own land when almost all the rest of their land was taken away from them? And who am I to complain when I myself stay on these properties? I like staying at Native American casinos because they provide relatively cheap accommodations for the upscale hotel quality. Casino resorts make much of their money through gambling revenues, but because I do not gamble I do not pay the extra costs. I once tried gambling on a cruise ship, playing Roulette and using various strategies to win, but I lost at every round. I stopped once I lost twenty dollars and never gambled again. The only things I do not like about casinos are the smoking and the frenetic environment. As such, I do not stay in casinos as much as I used to.

At my check in, the receptionist asked me if I had ever stayed with them before. I told her that I was there four years prior, and she found me in their system. I went up to my room on the tenth floor, looked out at the view, and then crashed into bed. The restlessness from my previous days' driving had finally caught up to me. It was right after 3 PM when I checked in and I fell hard asleep until 6. Later that evening, I went to have dinner. I drove 25 minutes to Scottsdale, hearing that this was a nice upscale community with shops. I made it to Fifth Street and the boutiques in that area, going into one of them that was still open by the time I got there at 8 PM. There was a nice older lady there who told me she was from Philadelphia. I told her that I was just there. I asked her about Arizona and she told me the people were not so nice, but that she liked living there because even though it got hot, it was not humid like Philadelphia. I told her how I found Philadelphia uncomfortably humid even in October.

Despite my long nap, I was still tired at a relatively early hour of night. I called my parents a little after 10 PM and right after that I went to sleep. I woke up at

6:15 the next morning before the sun had come up. I told myself that I had gotten enough sleep so I decided to leave my hotel that minute and make it to L.A. before rush hour. I had a short drive to the east before I got on the freeway and told myself I needed to make it there before the sun would come up. I did- right on time. I had a fast drive down the freeway the first mile, but then all of a sudden I hit bumper to bumper traffic. It was the morning rush hour of people driving into Phoenix. While that area had seen a major growth in freeway construction in recent years, the one bypassing the city to the southwest was still more than a month from opening. As such, I did what I do in L.A. I got off the freeway and took surface roads. I found myself on a maze of semi-main roads going past an endless collection of new houses with unnatural green lawns. Then I made my way onto Southern Boulevard going through the poorer parts of Phoenix before turning north somewhere past Central Avenue to get me on the freeway past downtown and thus in the opposite direction of the commuters.

I stopped at a restaurant in Quartzite for a pancake breakfast. The waitress there was not too nice. A couple hours later, I made a brief stop in Palm Springs. I used to go to that town on vacations with my parents and I very much liked all of its midcentury modern architecture. I had not been there in more than a decade, but Palm Springs did now seem like a very artsy town with a lot of eccentrics. My mother once suggested that I move there if I wanted a small place that was upscale but not too expensive. However, it was a bit too hot for me, even on that November day.

I liked the drive through the desert, with its near lack of cell towers, but once I would pass between the mountains just west of Palm Springs, I would be back in the L.A. metropolitan area with a cell tower at every mile of the freeway. I was not looking forward.

It was maybe not so much the cell towers as it was the traffic. Once I got into Anaheim, the traffic was unbearable and I got off the freeway. In New York, I drove on the freeways at 2:30 and the traffic was still not jammed. Here, even though the population was a bit smaller, it was not yet 1 PM and the traffic was jammed. I made my way through a network of surface roads before settling on the not too jammed 105 freeway. Driving down these L.A. freeways that I had long been familiar with, I realized that I had made it from New York to the South to the Old West and now I had found myself back in L.A. The feeling was quite overwhelming. Also now when I was hearing people talk about various places in the United States, or seeing the names of these places on restaurants, I would tell myself that I had actually been there, and that I had actually just gotten back from there.

I continued down the 105 past LAX, where many of my trips in the era when I still flew ended. I drove down the stretch of the freeway with the 1970s era aerospace highrises looming above the road across from the airport and appearing like a retro vision of the future. The freeway soon exited onto Imperial Highway and I drove a couple miles down that road until it ended at the Pacific Ocean. I had driven all the way across the country and back. Now all I had to do was drive a couple miles south on Vista Del Mar to get back to Manhattan Beach.

I got into the parking lot below the Metlox Plaza a few blocks from the ocean where I began my drive. My odometer read 7576 miles since I began my trip 23 days earlier that took me across 23 states. I walked up the stairs of the parking lot and then walked into Honeycomb, telling all my friends that I was back. They were all very excited that I had actually done that trip. I was also happy to see them and to be back, even though I was back in the land of heavy cell phone use. I made my way down Manhattan Beach Boulevard toward the ocean seeing my friends at the other stores. After having lunch at El Sombrero, there was only one thing left to do- walk down to the ocean to officially complete my trip. I walked onto the beach where I had so many encounters with my friends, where I had been with Hailey right before I started the trip, where people once gave me a hard time because of who I was hanging out with. I walked out to the edge of the ocean, dipped my feet in the water, and then bent down to put my hands in the water. My trip was complete. I had made it from the Pacific to the Atlantic and back to the Pacific, from Manhattan to Manhattan and back to Manhattan, from Los Angeles to New York and all the way back, all the way across the United States and back. That evening, I went to my parents' for dinner. Then I drove back to my house in Oxnard. My trip was done.

IX.   Back in Southern California

I was still planning on going back to West Virginia and getting a house there, but my parents were not being supportive, especially my father did not want me to buy a house there. The houses around Green Bank did not sell well and he did not want me to move there, decide I don't like that place, and then be stuck with the house when I would decide to move. Indeed I did not want to buy a house before I was sure I wanted to stay there, and preferred to rent first. The problem was that there were almost no rentals in that area. I could possibly rent a room at someone's house, but living with someone whom I did not know I would get along with would not work for me. The real estate agent suggested getting a rental from the Observatory, but these were generally not available to anyone not working there. There were a couple apartments in Marlinton, but none of them were of good quality. There were some Airbnbs in the area that looked good from the pictures, but I could never trust these properties. That left me with the hotel where I stayed. I heard people were allowed to stay there long term at discounted rates, but when I asked the owner about this, she told me she could only give me a 30 percent discount, and that my room would still be an expensive 100 dollars a night.

All this caused my parents to try to stop me from moving, and my dad said he would not pay for a house there. I told him that that was my human right to move to a place with no cell phone radiation. He would not accept that argument, however. I told him yes it was my human right to move to such a place. If I am injured by an environmental toxin and there is a place I can move to where that toxin has little or no presence and it is not too expensive to live there, it is my human right to move there. It was also my human right to not be denied moving somewhere that other adults without a disability were not denied moving to. I suggested that I only go stay at the hotel for a month, or possibly less time, and then I would for sure know if it was a place I wanted to move to.

I soon realized that I was back in the same place now. Not only was I back to the radiation migraines, I was back at a house where my neighbors' dogs barked really loudly, and it seemed to only have gotten worse since my trip. On some days they would start barking at seven in the morning and continue on until ten at night. No matter how tired I was, I would be awakened by the dogs, and then whenever I struggled to fall back asleep they would again start barking and wake me up. Adjusting my sleep cycle did not help much, as there was not a wide window where the dogs did not bark and I could not always fall asleep in time to get a full eight hours' sleep. When my parents and I complained to the neighbors, they ignored us, made empty promises to keep their dogs under control, or even complained that I was the one bothering them.

I was also back at a place where people stood me up for lunch after driving nearly two hours to Manhattan Beach. I was back at a place where promises and plans had little regard for people, particularly when it entailed going to eat with an older guy who had Asperger's. They would sound all excited about having lunch with me. I also got excited we were going to have lunch, as I did not have too many friends. But then right before we were to go they abruptly canceled on me. When I would try to reschedule, they would either tell me "maybe next week" and not honor that, or they would ignore me. They would say they were busy with school or with working multiple jobs, but that was still not a reason to make plans and then cancel them. Getting a thirty minute lunch does not take up so much of your time where you cannot honor your word, or at least reschedule in a timely manner, even if your schedule is a little busy. And they did have time to do these things with their other friends, on whom they did not flake out nearly as much. They just found me a less worthy person with whom to honor plans. Maybe they had their good friends with whom they met up all the time, but I did not have those good friends. I felt I was being treated as a second class citizen.

Even Stasia could no longer meet up with me for meals as much. In December, she underwent gastric bypass surgery, which meant she would no longer have an appetite for large meals at restaurants. She said she would still go sit down with me while I ate, but I doubted how much she would want to do that when she had her busy schedule and no appetite for the food. Marie did honor her word and got lunch with me when she came home for winter break, but she would go back to Texas soon. If I was not going to get married and make big sacrifices in my life for someone else, if I was not satisfied with being alone almost all the time, I needed a change of place.

Then there was someone named Monica. She kept telling me she would have dinner with me, but when I got to the restaurant she was nowhere to be found. She would message me about two hours before telling me something came up, but since I did not have a phone I did not get the message. Even if I did have a phone, that would not work. I would leave Oxnard more like four hours before our dinner so that I would avoid traffic and would hang out with my friends at the other stores until dinner. While I did enjoy hanging out with these friends, on many days I only went there because someone said she would get dinner with me and otherwise I was too tired to drive out there. Then on Monday February 3rd it happened again. I stayed in Manhattan Beach long after the stores closed. Then I got to the restaurant, waited in the cold for Monica to come, dodged people on their cell phones walking in and out of the restaurant, looked out to see if the next person coming was Monica, and left after more than half an hour with her being nowhere in sight. This was the third time in less than one month she did that to me. I got back home, checked my messages, there was no message from Monica this time. I wrote to her that I waited for her. She saw the message a few minutes later, but she never responded. It was at that moment that I decided I needed to leave Southern California.

X.   To West Virginia, again

I prepared to leave right the next day. I called my parents telling them I was going to do that, but again they tried to stop me. Indeed, by the time I was prepared to leave that day, it was getting a bit late, so I would wait until the next day. The following day, I got off to a bit of a late start and I did not leave until 2 PM. I was planning on going to see my parents and driving to Manhattan Beach, but I did not have time for that if I did not want to be stuck in L.A. rush hour traffic. I considered driving out to the ocean by my house, but I decided I did not need that formality if I had already been to the ocean since my last drive back. Rather, I only went to the Francesca's store in Oxnard where I had a couple friends. For the Manhattan Beach friends, I DM'd two of them telling them I was going on my road trip. Also, I posted the song "By the Time I Get to Phoenix" on my Facebook. Like the person in that song, I was leaving Southern California, taking almost the exact same route the narrator was taking, and the people I left did not believe I was actually going to do it.

The date was February 5th 2020. Donald Trump was cleared of impeachment charges that day. Kobe Bryant died in a helicopter crash not far from my house the previous week. The Coronavirus was shutting down Wuhan and other parts of China and some people feared it was coming to the U.S.

I took highway 126, the 14 freeway, and Pearblossom Highway- a network of roads that go just north of the mountains that delimit L.A.'s metropolitan core. I got back over the mountains in San Bernardino, where I stopped at Del Taco for a late lunch. As I stood in line, I tried to order the Taco Tuesday special. However, once I ordered that I was told that it was Wednesday. I had been so stressed out that I was forgetting what day of the week it was. I was now back in a more populated area and when I got back on the freeway in rush hour traffic it was jammed. Again, I got off the 210 freeway, got on to surface streets, got on the 10 freeway, got off when that was jammed also, and got back on the 10 freeway once I passed the urban area. I sped through the Palm Springs area, listening to the euro dance music on the LGBTQ friendly KGAY radio station that I discovered on my previous road trip.

I stopped for dinner at a McDonald's in Quartzsite right over the Arizona border. Normally I don't do fast food, but when I do not have much time and not too many places are open late at night, I will do the unhealthy fast food. The McDonald's was a bit too crowded for my tastes, even at 10 PM, but I found a quiet spot away from people on their phones. There was a long haired old guy who started talking to me. I asked him if he was a local and he told me he was.

He told me he had also left L.A. and moved there because it was cheaper and less crowded. I asked him if he liked living there and he told me he did. I told him "I'm looking for a place where the people are nice." He asked me "Am I nice?" I told him "You are." Then I told him "I am looking for a place where people are not on their phones all the time." He asked me "Am I on my phone?" He wasn't, but other people in that McDonald's were. Then I told him "I am looking for a place that doesn't get to hot." He told me "It only gets up to 128 over here." I told him "When it's 90 degrees it's already too hot for me." Quartzsite would not be the place for me.

I got to my hotel in the suburbs of Phoenix right after midnight, though it was only 11 PM for me because I came from Pacific Time. The following morning I drove to Downtown Phoenix just to see it before getting on the freeway. Downtown is not the most exciting part of Phoenix- it is merely an inane collection of tall buildings. Driving on the 60 freeway through Mesa, I was being bombarded by the multitude of powerful cell towers, but that soon cleared once I got out of the metropolitan area and back to the stretch of the 60 that went through the mountains. I continued to Globe, but instead of turning onto U.S. 70 to retrace the drive from my previous trip, I stayed on the 60 going deeper and higher up into the mountains and driving past some spectacular scenery on a road that had almost no traffic. I was thinking to myself of all the hurt I suffered from my friends standing me up and that I did not want to go back to that environment. Then I got a speeding ticket, one on a very lightly traveled road that was the last place I would expect a police officer waiting for me and checking my speed.

Over the New Mexico border, I stopped at Pie Town. I had read about someone who biked across the country on the same road I was taking and who stopped at that town, so I had to stop there also. Pie Town is really only a couple houses and a restaurant that sells- you guessed it- pies. I got an apple pie a la mode for lunch, and it was quite good. Soon I passed by the National Radio Astronomical Observatory of New Mexico. It is a collection of dishes very similar to the array in Green Bank. No quiet zone is established around these dishes, but there is no need for one- no house is found within ten miles of the observatory and the nearest sizable town is more than twenty miles away.

The clouds had a spectacular fire red glow after sunset that day. I was heading into the mountains to the town of Ruidoso, located at an elevation of 7000 feet. A friend of mine from Mensa told me she was there once and I should check out that place if I wanted a quiet place with nice people. Driving there was a bit treacherous. I was taking the back way, as that was more along my route, and as

I drove up the mountains it started snowing and there was black ice on the road. My car stalled at one point and I started getting worried that my car would not make it. Luckily it was only at that one point and I soon arrived at my hotel in Ruidoso. The people at the check in seemed nice and they all told me they liked living in that town.

The following morning I called my mother after not having spoken to her since I left Oxnard. She asked me how was I doing. Then she told me there would be some rough weather on my way and that there was a tornado watch in Alabama. I told her if that would be the case I would go around these areas, or maybe stay at a hotel on the way for a few days. My mother begged me to come back home.

I decided I would continue at least to Fort Worth for my planned breakfast with Marie the following day, the girl on whom I could rely not to flake on me. I did not want to take a long look at the weather now, as the public computer at the hotel only had wireless Internet. I would check it at a library on my way. First I went into downtown Ruidoso to see how the people there were. The people at the stores were a bit on the more grumpy side, and there were quite a lot of dogs and cell phones. I would not be moving to that town. I continued to Roswell, the city with the purported alien crash-landing. I went to the public library, looked up the tornado watch, and saw that it was over. I looked at the weather forecast for the places on my way, and they were all supposed to have good weather for the days I would drive through them. Some of these places would have snow and storms, including West Virginia, but only a week later and after my arrival date. I e-mailed my parents saying that I was continuing. I also joked with them that because I was In Roswell maybe I would take the opportunity to move to another planet.

The whole town capitalizes on the purported "Roswell Incident". Sculptures and drawings of extraterrestrials are found all over Main Street, and there is a McDonald's where part of the building looks like a UFO. The town's motto was "We Believe", and it appeared on signs outside the Visitor Center. I asked someone there if people there really thought extraterrestrials landed there. He told me it is about half and half. When I asked that question of someone at the UFO Museum, she told me "That's what they say". Personally, I do believe something happened in Roswell that July day in 1947, something the Government still does not want to admit to. I do not think it was a weather balloon, as the official explanation goes, but it was not extraterrestrials either. It was most likely a military experiment involving beings on Earth, and it is very logical why such a thing would occur at that place and time. It happened in New Mexico, the same state where the Manhattan Project was done. It happened in a sparsely populated area where there would not be too many witnesses or risk of property damage. There was a military base there, and we already know the incident was connected to the base, even under the alien hypothesis. It happened right after the end of World War II and the Manhattan Project, and right on the eve of the Cold War. What very likely happened was that the military was developing a secret experimental aircraft and/or weapon of a nature the military still does not want to divulge, and that aircraft crashed in the desert near Roswell. Believers say it was extraterrestrials but the Government doesn't want you to know that. I think it is the other way around. It was not extraterrestrials, but the Government wants you to believe it was- at least they benefit from people believing that, as it detracts from people questioning what might have really happened.

As for the existence of life elsewhere in the universe, I do very much believe that exists. In a universe 27 billion light years across, there is little doubt that Earth is not the only place where life exists, or even the only place where intelligent life exists. I do not believe any of this life has ever reached Earth, however. There is no intelligent life elsewhere in the Solar System, and the closest star with planets to our Solar System is more than four light years away. If beings from one of that star's planets were to travel to Earth at one thousandth the speed of light, 670 000 miles per hour and already nearly thirty times faster than the fastest space shuttles built on Earth, it would take more than 4000 years to reach Earth. It would be nearly impossible for any vehicle to support the physical needs of complex intelligent beings for that amount of time. Even if such a vehicle would be possible by a civilization on a planet in that star's system, the odds that even life as intelligent as Earth's exists over there are very slim. I do, however, hear that life may exist in the underground lakes of a moon of Saturn where liquid water is likely to exist. Some scientists theorize that it may be possible for life to exist at much colder temperatures than previously thought and that it may exist on other moons of Saturn that are covered with liquid methane at a temperature of negative 200 degrees Celsius. However, Saturn is still much farther than any human beings have traveled, and the science about intelligent life being possible on these moons is highly questionable.

After Roswell, I continued down a seventy mile stretch of desert with not a single town until I got into Texas. That was where the scenery changed to dry farmland and towns began appearing at regular twenty mile intervals. Now that I was passing that landscape in the daytime, I could pay attention to the vegetation that was gradually getting denser the farther east I was going. By 7 PM I made it back to Abilene. This time I went to downtown, a nice part of town, for dinner.

A couple restaurants I tried going to were very crowded that Friday night, but I soon found a restaurant in a historic building that was a bit expensive but did not have way too many people. I noticed that people there really did not use their cell phones as much as they did in Southern California, not even the young people. They sat down and enjoyed their food and company. It was only a couple of people dining alone who spent much time on their phones.

I got to my hotel between Dallas and Fort Worth at around 10. I checked my messages. Marie was confirming we would meet the following day, and I was happy she was still on. We met the following morning at a restaurant by the river in Fort Worth. We took a short walk by the river right after breakfast, with me often having to detour around the dogs. She told me she would love to meet with me on my return drive, but I told her I would probably not be coming through Texas on that drive- I wanted to see St. Louis. She gave me a hug before we parted. That was one of the last hugs I got before the pandemic.

After breakfast, I went back east on the freeways in good spirits. I did not need to go back on the streets of Downtown Dallas, having seen that the previous time. Rather, I got off on U.S. 80 once I passed the metropolitan area. U.S. 80 was known as the Broadway of America, and indeed much of that highway was wide, even the stretches passing through the old towns that could not be widened for modern traffic. I stopped in Mineola, a colorful town of brick buildings, and walked around their downtown. I parked by a plaque commemorating the town's Jewish merchants, and indeed when I walked into an antique store, I found an elderly salesman with a heavy Eastern European accent having menorahs behind the counter. I asked him if he was Jewish and he told me he was. He was a very friendly person with whom I spent a good twenty minutes chatting. I asked him what brought him out to that remote corner of Texas. He told me he used to live in New York and that his wife brought him there. I asked him if there was a lot of anti-Semitism there. His response was that there is anti-Semitism everywhere.

I got back in the Interstate forty miles later when U.S. 80 rejoined I-20. I got back off after I crossed into Louisiana and was in the outskirts of Shreveport. I had a black aide in my class when I was in fifth grade who was born in that town but moved to the other L.A.- Los Angeles- when she was a little girl. While driving to Shreveport, I was thinking of what it was like for her family to be driving in the 1940s down some of the very same roads I was taking, moving to a new place to live, and not being able to stop everywhere because of the color of their skin.

Driving through Shreveport, I could understand why so many people left that place. This was probably the most neglected large city I had even seen in the United States. A few other cities might me more neglected, but I had never been to them yet. The old highway leading to downtown was lined with brick buildings in various states of disrepair. Some of them were completely hollowed out leaving only part of the exterior walls intact. It looked like the ruins of an ancient civilization, but this was a living U.S. city. Downtown was a bit better, having some glistening modern tall office buildings and casinos along the river, but still on the radio whenever there were advertisements for things in the Shreveport area, they always mentioned its suburb of Bossier City in addition, and sometimes said its name before Shreveport.

I continued on U.S. 80 through the small town of Minden, where a fair was going on. I was trying to find a place to have lunch, as it was getting quite late in the day. I found a newly built restaurant just outside of Minden where the old highway intersected with a more modern surface expressway. I got some fried catfish, a Louisiana staple. The food was not bad, but once I got back to California and ate at my favorite Cajun restaurant in Redondo Beach, I realized the food there was way better. Just because a food item originated in a certain region or is most popular in a certain region does not mean it will always be best prepared in that region. But then again that way Northern part of Louisiana was not quite bayou country. I am sure they have some wonderful fish fries farther south.

After my late lunch, I continued back on the old highway for another half hour until sunset, when I got on the Interstate. Once I got on the freeway, I saw a motorist pulled over by the police. I was so happy I did not speed since Arizona, even though I was tempted to do it sometimes.

My original plan was to drive that day to Jackson, Mississippi, but the previous night when I did my research, I saw it was too far from Dallas if I wanted to take the old highways and still not arrive at my hotel at 10 PM. As such, I looked for other places that were a bit closer. That was when I found Vicksburg, the site of the Civil War battle. I reserved a room at an antebellum mansion turned bed and breakfast.

Driving down the Interstate now, I was counting the miles to that moment where I would cross the Mississippi and be in Vicksburg. I estimated I would be there at 7:45 and, being exhausted, I hoped I would not need to drive far from the freeway to get to my hotel.

The hotel turned out to be about three miles from the freeway. I passed through various historic neighborhoods and interesting roads to get there, though I could not see much because it was dark. I realized that I forgot to print out a street map of the hotel's area or even write down the address. All I remembered was that it was in the old part of town and that it was in the northwest portion a couple blocks south of where the town ends at the battlefield and a couple blocks east of where it ends at the river. But then again that was enough to narrow it down for me, I figured.

I drove to the edge of town, going block by block looking for my hotel, but there was no sign of it. I tried going into a gas station to ask for directions, but it was busy with people going in and out of the door- and on their phones. As such, I went back to where I was before, driving down the steep hills to the river and then back up, but could not find my hotel. I thought it might be in a different neighborhood, so I went farther south and practically saw the whole town now-the historic courthouse, Washington Street with its shops and tall brick buildings, the restaurants by the river. I got to the fire station. The gates were open, so I walked in trying to ask someone for directions, but I could not find anyone. Then I made it to the Ameristar Casino. I was going to use the computers there to find my hotel, but before I could do that someone gave me a Vicksburg visitor's guide with a map. I could not find my hotel listed there either- I forgot its name. I drove back to the historic neighborhood where I was before, and now, after searching for half an hour, I finally found my hotel.

I checked myself in. My room was in the carriage house, a bit more affordable and plain than the main mansion but still well appointed. I wanted to take a long nap because I was so tired, but could not do so if I wanted to have dinner before the restaurants closed. I was going to eat at my hotel's critically acclaimed restaurant, but it was closed for the day. Instead, I made it back out to Washington Street. I saw they had a restaurant on the roof of one of the tall brick buildings and I decided to check it out. Frankly, I was a bit surprised to see these buildings that clearly dated from the early 20th century. I didn't know Vicksburg was such a large and prosperous place after the Civil War.

I was joined by two young women going up the elevator. They were going to one of the loft apartments that occupied the majority of that building now. I asked them if Vicksburg was a good place to live and they told me not really. That stretch along the river and the antebellum district were frankly the only parts of Vicksburg that seemed nice. This clearly was not Gettysburg with its college town vibe.

The restaurant was not completely packed, but it was a bit frenetic and difficult to find a seat away from people walking around on their phones. I did what I often do in these places. Whenever someone walks by on their phone, I run away from that person. Then if another person is on the phone I dodge that person also. It was 9 PM, an hour before closing, and I decided I would come back later when the crowds would die out. I went back to my hotel, took a quick rest, and came back at 9:40. The crowds were much thinner now. The place had a nice vibe now with the tenth story rooftop views of the city and the band playing nineties rock covers. I got an older woman as my waitress, and we talked quite a lot about my trip and her life. She told me she had moved there from Texas a couple years prior and had a twelve year old son with autism. We talked a lot about her son's problems at school and I told her all about the problems I had in school when I was his age. She then told me that the people at the restaurant asked for her to be my waitress because they realized I had some special needs when I was running away from people on their phones.

That is the difference between more liberal and more conservative places. In California, with the exception of professionals and law enforcement, people will not ask you about your special needs. They don't want to seem judgmental. But while not everyone is comfortable talking about one's special needs, the don't ask standard is not necessarily better. People still judge behind one's back. That woman in Mississippi, on the other hand, showed that she was with me. This is, however, not to say there is no prejudice against people with disabilities in the more conservative places. That woman's son still had eyes staring at him and was segregated from his non-disabled peers in special education.

Being a bed and breakfast, the morning meal was included with my stay. Since I was the only guest there, which I found quite surprising with it being the weekend, I was given my food in the library instead of the restaurant room. It is quite common in the South to turn antebellum mansions and plantations into bed and breakfasts, and sitting in the parlor of such a mansion waiting for my food to be served definitely felt unusual. It was like going back in time to another era-one that I found interesting but was not necessarily the most comfortable with. Nevertheless, there was a unique charm to this mansion and it is true what they say about Southern hospitality. After breakfast, I was taken on a tour of the mansion. The Anchuca House, as it is now called, was built in 1830 and during the Civil War was owned by the brother of Jefferson Davis. It was from that house's balcony that Jefferson Davis gave a farewell speech in 1869 before being hauled off to prison for war crimes. I visited the upstairs rooms, and found it unusual that the rooms in this museum house were often occupied by modern day guests who had access to flat screen TVs hidden behind the doors of wooden dressers. I went out to the courtyard with its magnolia trees that were just beginning to bloom.

After my tour, I drove out to the battlefield. My first stop there was the USS Cairo, not named after the city in Egypt but named after the one in Illinois that was in turn named for the one in Egypt. This was an ironclad warship that got sunk in the war not too far from Vicksburg, and which was discovered and raised a century later. What I found most interesting here was the ship's roster, which was shown in a picture on one of the display boards. Each crew member's hair, eye, and skin color was recorded, as well as the places they were from, and the crew was actually quite diverse. There were people from the British Isles and Germany as well as ones born in the United States. There were a few black members, a couple of Southern and Eastern Europeans, and a Hispanic from California. Skin color had more degradations than simply white, brown, and black. Among people who would generally be considered white now, there were fair, light, dark, and a couple others. Then there were a couple people whose color was listed as yellow or red. This made for an interesting anthropological study in the composition of the crew, the different appearances of people from different parts of the world, and the ways skin color that doesn't fall into straight categories of basic colors was visualized in different times.

Here is the brief history of the Battle of Vicksburg. In the spring of 1863, Confederate forces in Vicksburg began attacking civilian supply ships belonging to Union sailing up the Mississippi. The Union saw the river as a public highway, even as it passed through Confederate territory, and when the Confederate leaders did not agree to stop the attacks, the Union invaded Vicksburg and put the city under siege. A battle ensued and finally after forty days of siege the Confederate general agreed to surrender and the Union took over Vicksburg. The surrender happened one day after the Union victory at Gettysburg and for that reason these two Union victories are seen as the turning point of the Civil War.

While the Union might have been celebrating, the Confederate certainly were not. Since the defeat of the Confederate at Vicksburg happened on July 4th, Independence Day was not celebrated in that city for eighty years. I have mixed feelings about the feelings some white Southerners still have about the loss of the Confederacy. They lost a war. Their nation got crushed. Their economy got ruined. Many people died. No matter on which side you are on, it cannot be dismissed that especially the last of these things was a tragedy. The vast majority of the people flying Confederate flags do not want to see a return to slavery. Even the Civil War was not entirely fought over slavery. States rights and low taxes were also important issues. However, Confederate symbols do represent a side that does not believe in civil rights and integration too much. Even if people displaying them do not believe in slavery, they do represent a system that oppresses people based on the color of their skin. Germany also lost many people during World War II and had its economy ruined, but you do not have too many people there flying Nazi flags and you do not see monuments to Nazi generals in the streets. Yes, maybe we could have solved the issue of slavery without having as many people die. Yes, maybe the Southern economy did not need to get ruined as much by the abolition of slavery. However, just because many people died for a certain cause does not mean they died for the right one. And the Union did help rebuild the South and its economy after it was crushed in the war. The idea of antebellum Southern prosperity is little more than romanticized history conjured up by a poor region. That wealth was only concentrated among a small percentage of the population who owned large plantations. Most of the blacks there, whether free or enslaved, were dirt poor. I do not generally support bans on Confederate flags and symbols- that is a violation of freedom of speech- but I don't think highly of people who display them for non-historic purposes either.

I drove on the park road past the monuments erected by the states to their soldiers who participated in the battle. Some states had very ornate monuments- Illinois had a whole enclosed rotunda- other states had very simple ones. Some had tall granite columns with statues of classical symbols. As a testimony to the poverty of many Southern states, some of them did not erect monuments until the second half of the 20th century, and this is evident in the much more modern style these monuments have. The battlefield roads also had many joggers taking advantage of the unseasonably warm day for their exercise.

I spent a bit more time at the battlefield than I intended. This was the day of the Oscars and being from Los Angeles this was quite a big thing for me. I wanted to be at my hotel in Chattanooga in time to watch the broadcast from the beginning, but neither did I want to skimp on sightseeing. I got back on old U.S. 80 driving through the forests and small towns of that part of Mississippi, passing by houses with large black families gathered on their front porches in a scene widely depicted of that area. The 90s song "Black Velvet" came on the radio. "Mississippi in the middle of a dry spell..." I had heard that song many times on the radio before, but never before had I actually heard it in Mississippi. I was debating whether to reenter the interstate to save time, especially when the old highway ran right next to it. I finally entered the freeway right by a gas station run by an Indian guy where I stopped to get a soda.

I got off the freeway twenty miles later to drive through Jackson. I wanted to drive through downtown, but it was not until after I passed the roads leading to the tall buildings that I realized U.S. 80 bypasses downtown. I made a u-turn and then turned onto U.S. 51. In downtown I turned onto the main streets and drove past the Mississippi State Capitol, giving myself an express tour of the city. I did not step out of my car- I did not have the time and frankly the city was not too interesting. I immediately got back on the freeway and past the town to get onto the Natchez Parkway. My plan was to take that road to Tupelo and visit the house where Elvis was born.

That portion of the Natchez Trace Parkway was not nearly as interesting as the one I took on my previous trip. The scenery was nice but repetitive. Also, the speed limit was quite low and I did not want to risk another ticket by going past it. Then I came upon an RV that was going even slower and with no room to pass it. I did not know now if I could get to Elvis's house before it closed, and if I would go there I would surely miss the Oscars. I knew I could catch them online later, but like a sporting event, I wanted to see it live when the Best Picture Oscar was handed. I soon got off the parkway and would not go to Tupelo.

I now took the rather lackluster Mississippi Highway 16. Passing through the town of Carthage, I was looking for a place to have lunch. I drove to the square by the courthouse, but any of the few places that were there were closed because it was Sunday. I got back on the main highway and soon passed a roadside buffet place. I got there right in the nick of time before they closed at 3 PM. I helped myself to fried chicken and an apple crumb pie, which were very good. The highway was only two lanes, but then all of a sudden it became a wide four lane road with light poles on either side. I realized I had entered the Choctaw Reservation and soon I passed an out of place 20 story casino resort. I continued through the town of Philadelphia, same name as the one with the Liberty Bell and the one by which my aunt lives, but completely different place. Soon I crossed into Alabama. Ever since my previous road trip where I randomly crossed into that state I had dreams that I was somehow back in Alabama. Now it had come true.

I got on the freeway at my first opportunity. That part of the state was very lackluster and I wanted to get to my hotel as soon as possible. After nightfall, I was driving through Birmingham, an interesting place to see in Alabama. I wanted to again get out at the edge of town and drive through the city on the streets, but I did not have the time and I satisfied myself with seeing the city from the freeway. It looked a bit like Pittsburgh with its rolling hills. Like Pittsburgh, it used to be a steel town. I decided to at least get off in downtown and go past the Civil Rights National Monument, which was what I did now. I could not find the Civil Rights place (it turned out I only missed it by one block), but I did give myself a brief tour of downtown. I parked my car when I got to a street of restaurants and shops and was going to get out, but the area was unappealing. It was not run down, but there was not really any life there. It was now 7 PM, or 5 PM Pacific Time, the start time of the Oscars, and Chattanooga was still two hours away. Seeing the tall hotels in downtown Birmingham, I wished I could stay there instead, but I already had my reservations for Chattanooga.

I continued on U.S. 11 for a few miles until the freeway crossed it, passing through a heavy industrial area and inner city neighborhoods. I am sure Birmingham has some nicer areas, but later I read that Birmingham ranks in the 97th percentile for most crime ridden cities in the United States. Rain was starting to fall, and it grew heavy at times on my drive. I heard on the radio that it was also raining at the Oscars. I got to my hotel right after 10 Eastern Time, 9 Central Time, and this time it was easy to find. It was a tall building right off the freeway in downtown.

I checked myself in and got up to my room in time to watch Elton John performing his song from *Rocketman*, which would win the Oscar for Best Original Song. I ordered room service, knowing once the Oscars would be over the restaurants would be closed. I ate that in my room with a view of the TVA building while watching what remained of the ceremony. When Billie Eilish came on stage with her black and green hair, I called my room key the "Billie Eilish Key" because it was also black but with a green stripe. The Best Picture win I found quite shocking, being the Korean psychological thriller Parasite. I am not much of a fan of that genre. I find it too scary and depressing. However, I was glad for all the Koreans who broke the cultural barriers in winning Best Picture.

I was now thirsty from my food. I went to the hotel's market to get a drink. Here it was not only the vending machines on the room floors that only had water, the hotel's marketplace also only had water and low calorie drinks that basically taste like highly watered down soft drinks. They also had teas and coffees, but they have caffeine and are not good for someone trying to go to sleep. So just like in Russia, I would need to travel now to find a drink of my choice. I tried going to Walmart, but the freeway onramps were closed due to construction and now I didn't know how to get there. I drove along the river trying to find a gas station or a grocery store, but I found none. Finally, after twenty minutes of driving, I went into another hotel on the river and got myself three juice bottles at an inflated price. I also took that opportunity to check my messages, as the public computers there had a wired connection.

I had long associated Chattanooga with the Chattanooga Choo Choo song. I also associated it with ice packs, which I used to call Chattanoogas. The first time I saw the name of that place was on an ice pack I had as a child that was manufactured there. Chattanooga did indeed have a long manufacturing history, and was still home to many breweries and distilleries. I called it the Portland of Tennessee, also due to it having a hipster scene and being a bit more liberal than the rest of the state.

I was very tired of driving all day for five days straight. Though I could in theory make it to my hotel in West Virginia in one day, I did not want to arrive late and have the same dinner problem as last time. As such, I gave myself a break by only driving two hours and reserving a hotel in Knoxville. That gave me some time to explore the Portland of Tennessee. I went to Lookout Mountain. I was going to go to the summit to see the view, but it was too foggy. Instead, I went to Ruby Falls, an underground waterfall.

That place was only discovered in 1929, and we were shown a movie about its discovery on our tour. The person who owned the hillside liked spending time in a cave at the base of the mountain. But then the railroad got expanded and they needed to seal off the entrance to the cave. Not wanting to lose access, he built an elevator shaft from his property going 420 feet down into the cave. Then when he got to the 260 foot level he was hit by a gush of air and water. He realized he had come upon another cave, one that was only a foot and a half high. He figured there was likely something spectacular inside, so he went crawling in through that tube. Several hours later, he came upon a place where he could stand up and he found cave rooms with stalactites. Farther down, however, was the most spectacular thing inside- a waterfall inside a cave towering 145 feet high!

While he did build the elevator down to the original cave, this newly discovered cave would be his money maker. He spent the next year digging out the floor of the cave so that it would be tall enough for tourist to stand inside. At a little more than six feet, it was now barely enough for the average person to stand inside. Our guide told us about a 6 foot 11 inches guy who had gone on his tour recently and had to bend down for much of it.

These low ceilinged passages were definitely a bit claustrophobic, so I walked either at the front or at the back of my group. I was also a bit afraid of the lights going out. Though I was assured they would not turn them off, I was afraid of there being a blackout. But I also knew there were flashlights and emergency lights just in case. Once we got out of the low ceilinged passageways, the formations were quite spectacular. There were stalactites on the ceiling and ponds with water that were lit with blue and red spotlights in such a way that, made the place look like a Disney dark ride or Elsa's cave from *Frozen*. It was like Carlsbad Caverns, but on a smaller scale and with less natural looking light.

Twenty minutes and nearly half a mile later, we entered the room with the waterfall. We were now 1100 feet underground (we were under a higher part of the mountain now) and I could not believe such a waterfall existed underground, This was a cave room with nearly smooth walls, like something out of a Jules Verne novel. This place did not seem natural. It seemed like someone decided to hollow out a room within a rock and put in this waterfall. The cave and waterfall are indeed natural, but according to Wikipedia the waterfall room was apparently hollowed out at one point to give people a better view of the falls. Another thing not natural here were the lights shining on the waterfall. The falls were bathed in red light, which then turned to green, blue, purple, and white- not necessarily in that order. This show was very well orchestrated along with the dramatic music playing from the speakers.

After the waterfall, I headed back into the city and then took U.S. 11 out the other way in the direction of Knoxville. I was looking for a place to have lunch, and a little past downtown and the tunnel I found a place serving hot chicken that apparently was featured on food shows. It seemed good so I decided to check it out. It was not too busy inside, but ahead of me there was someone taking a long time with her complex order. I always hate it when that happens. When you have a simple order to make, you should not be made to wait ten minutes for someone else to finish her more complex order just because she arrived first. That is not fair to the person whose order should only take one minute. I walked out of that place, as I have done from other places where I had this situation, but then I decided to come back. I didn't want to be stuck with a McDonald's when I could have the good chicken in that place. When they were finally ready to take my order, I got my chicken medium. They asked me if I had been there before and I told them no. They said that if I was not used to that place I should get the mild, as the medium there was REALLY spicy. I got the mild. That was quite intensely spicy- definitely not what you would expect mild to be anywhere else- but it was still edible, and very tasty. That was probably the best food I had on this road trip.

I got to Knoxville at around five that afternoon. If Chattanooga is the Portland of Tennessee, Knoxville is the New York of Tennessee. Like the Big Apple, it has a very urban feel (at least in the downtown) with tall brownstone buildings. It also has a theatre district centered along a street with the rather unusual name of Gay. That was the street on which my hotel was located. I was staying in the century old ten story building that was the Hyatt Place, but which originally was the Farragut, one of the city's most distinguished hotels until it closed in the 1960s. It was offices for many years, but had reopened as a hotel in the 2010s with its lobby beautifully restored to its early 20th century appearance. I got up to my hotel room. Exhausted from my six days of driving without getting enough sleep, I crashed onto my bed. Two hours later, after satisfying myself with my nap, I got up to have dinner. I walked down Gay Street looking for a place to eat and found a Vietnamese deli. I ordered my food, but was told I would need to take it to go, as the restaurant was a few minutes from closing. I had no idea that a month later all restaurants would be like that.

The following day I was finally ready to go to West Virginia and to the hotel where I stayed last time. I called them in the morning letting them know I would be arriving that day. The person whom I spoke to did not know me- she wasn't there at my previous stay and told me she would be happy to meet me now. I was wondering whether this driving across the country looking for a house in West Virginia and then driving back to L.A. to visit my parents would become the new normal. It definitely seemed that way now, as this was the normal for me a few years earlier when I drove from Oregon to L.A. and back every month. Except now the drive would be nearly all the way across the country instead of just to the neighboring state. I got very excited once I crossed into West Virginia that afternoon. Maybe this was a poor state, one that was far from where I grew up, but I was happy to be back there among the beautiful mountains and people who were not glued to their phones.

XI. Back in the WV

I had learned my lesson from the previous trip and now stopped for dinner in Lewisburg, going to the Chinese place by the freeway. It was 6:40 PM, only an hour before the time I arrived there on my first trip, so I was not too happy about that. But it was still early enough to make it to the hotel when the people were still awake. I was not too sure whether I wanted to move back to West Virginia, but as soon as I got up highway 92 into the mountains towards my hotel it became more clear. The migraines I had experienced throughout the trip and in California had suddenly gone away. I was just in a wireless radiation heavy environment that was the Chinese restaurant and only half an hour later my headaches were completely gone. I was feeling much better than I had felt anywhere else for a long time, and I knew I needed to move to such a place.

I drove back down the dark dirt road leading to the main building of the hotel. I looked inside the building where the front office was. A couple lights were on but I did not see anyone there. I opened the door and called out for the person at the desk. The new person called out saying she would be right there. Then I heard a dog barking. There were no dogs at the hotel the previous time and I was wondering what that was. Then when the office lady finally came down her dog came to greet me and I closed the door behind me telling her "Make sure the dog does not come up to me!" She told me that the dog was very nice and would not hurt me. I told her I did not want to get licked. She assured me her dog did not lick. I told her that I still did not want the dog coming up to me.

She agreed to put the dog up that one time so that I could come in and pay for my room. She told me she did not see me the previous time because she was driving back from Vancouver then to pick up her dog. The Utahn was not there-he had gone back home until April. She told me that since I would be staying there for a whole month, her dog and I should become good friends and that we would grow to like each other. I now decided I would only pay for until the end of February, and that if I were to stay longer I would pay later. Even though she told me the dog would not lick me, and even though that and biting are the things I am more afraid of dogs doing to me, that does not work for me. For one thing, people are not always completely honest. Also, I do not want a dog "threatening" to lick me either. I do not want a dog nipping me, coming within two inches of me, or running after me with its body very close to me. This is something dog admirers do not always understand. I told her now that I came to West Virginia in part because I thought there would not have dogs all over the place. I was trying to get away from the attitudes that dogs can be loved more than people or that it is OK for people to let their dogs come up to other people whether they like it or not, and that everyone should like dogs. However, I was also staying at a hippie-ish hotel and complex. While hippies tend to be enlightened and have free spirited philosophies that align with mine, many of them are dog people.

When I got up to my room, I was wondering if I even wanted to stay one more night at that hotel if the office lady would let her dog run all over the main building. Fortunately for me, however, she went on a ten day vacation the day after I arrived and Casey was now the main person at the office. She was much more sympathetic to my concerns and made sure the dog stayed away from me. Apparently other people at the hotel were not comfortable with the dog walking all over the place either. Another electrosensitive working there told me she tried asking the office lady not to let her dog do that, but she wasn't receptive. As for Casey, she was not afraid of dogs, but not a huge fan or theirs either. My mom tried telling me that people out in nature would likely be very attached to dogs, but knowing that electrosensitives often have other sensitivities also, I figured many of them would not like dogs jumping on them either. Even though there were some who did like dogs, I now saw that about the rest of them I was right.

Casey did prove to be a very nice hostess. Nearly every day she invited me to hang out with her and her husband, who worked at the hotel as a handyman, as they cooked dinner. Then we all ate together, with their daughter joining in when she was not being a grumpy teenager. Sometimes we would have other electrosensitives living in the area visiting for dinner. Then there were the hotel guests, mostly people who came over the weekend to ski at Snowshoe. Some of these guests were very friendly, especially a woman originally from Los Angeles who also moved to West Virginia and who came to stay at the hotel with her daughter two weekends in a row because she liked it so much. All of this company helped me not feel alone.

Casey did not like working at the hotel too much, as they sometimes had to have the wi-fi on for the guests, but since I was usually the only one staying there when it was not the weekend, they did not have to turn it on. I remember one time they had to turn on the wi-fi for half an hour when all of us were in the dining room. Even though no one in the room was on their devices and the router was far from us and wrapped in a mesh to lessen the radiation, Casey and I soon started getting slight headaches. In the world outside the Quiet Zone, where I am constantly surrounded by wireless signals, I don't notice these things, but now that I was in a place with no wireless signals, my body did notice when a tiny wireless signal was turned on. Casey's husband, who was not particularly electrosensitive, also told me that he began noticing the way his body reacted to these signals after moving to the Quiet Zone.

I got back in touch with the real estate agent I had met on my previous trip and now I did some more househunting with him. The first house we saw was on the main highway and right up the road from Green Bank. It was Valentine's Day and it was snowing. The house had its charm and I liked the large lot size, but it was also more than a century old and not fixed up everywhere. I would need to look for more places. We went to a recently built house down a back road. It was not too expensive- only $250 000- and well built. The only problems were that it had too much wood and that it was too big for one person. The houses that seemed most appealing from the pictures were down a road called Erehwon. We went there now. The drive was quite intense, as the houses were four miles down an unpaved road in the snow. I wasn't sure whether I wanted these houses now, but I proceeded on. When I got to the homes and my agent got there in his car, I told him about my experience. He asked me if I knew what Erehwon means. I did. It's "nowhere" spelled backwards. The houses indeed did look nice, but it was too middle of nowhere for me, to put it lightly. The snow was very light that day and my car could handle it, but I did not know what I would do in heavier snow. My agent again told me that I should get a 4x4, but on such a road that might not have been enough for me either. I am the type of person who will drive out while a storm is raging if the alternative is to sit in a house in near total darkness due to a blackout.

We visited more places around Pocahontas County. Then I discovered the community of Slatyfork. That was where my agent lived and from the pictures the houses there appeared very nice and moderately priced. It was a bit outside the Quiet Zone, so my agent was not sure if it would be a good place for me, but it was still close enough to the Quiet Zone and the low population and the proximity to the Observatory meant that it was not likely they would install powerful cell towers anytime soon. My agent told me he would get cell service there when he would drive up the mountains, but that was it.

When I went to visit the houses, they were indeed all very well designed. They did not look like backwoods cabins, but rather like fancy ski chalets in Colorado. My agent told me that Slatyfork was considered an upscale area. It was indeed (almost) just what I was looking for. It was upscale, but the prices were low. I was happy that such a place existed in the area with low cell reception. The only problems were that there was no town center or places to hang out there and that many of the roads leading to the houses were unpaved.

Nevertheless, the roads were better maintained than the road to Erehwon and involved a shorter distance drive down the unpaved roads. I could live right up the mountain in Snowshoe. There were more paved roads and a bit more to do there, but that place was too cold and it was cell phone and wi-fi country.

I imagined myself living in Slatyfork and writing all sorts of works. In this low electromagnetic radiation where I could actually concentrate, I was thinking of a long James Michener type novel I might like to write about the history of West Virginia. It would deal with many different characters- both fictional and real-living in different time periods: The original Native American inhabitants, Native Americans who fled from farther east in Virginia when whites started settling, whites fleeing the strictures of society in Virginia, Civil War soldiers, loggers, coal miners, railroad workers, and finally the electrosensitives. Toward the end of the book, there would be a promising young West Virginian circa 1960 who cannot find a good engineering job in his home state so he moves to Southern California somewhere near Manhattan Beach to work in the aerospace industry. Then in 2019 there would be an electrosensitive hanging out in Manhattan Beach who gets flaked on by various people, including the granddaughter of this engineer, and then decides to move to West Virginia.

I soon settled into a routine. I would spend the days visiting houses, then go back to my hotel, take a long nap, and get up to have dinner with Casey and whomever else joined us. I also spent my time exploring the rest of Pocahontas County with its scenic mountain roads, streams, and the Greenbrier River that cut right through the heart of the county. Right next door was Greenbrier County with the town of Lewisburg, which now that I was staying in West Virginia longer I took the time to explore. This was a center of culture in an otherwise remote mountain area. The town had only 4000 people, but it had a great historic center with boutiques not too different from the ones in Manhattan Beach as well as quality restaurants. Nearby, I visited the historic Greenbrier Hotel. This was the Beverly Hills of West Virginia. Going into the property and seeing its corridor with boutiques of the like of Prada and Gucci made me feel like I was back in a wealthy part of L.A. instead of in one of the poorest U.S. states.

While in West Virginia, I also took the opportunity to sightsee farther afield. I drove out one day to the Blue Ridge Parkway, which was less than two hours from my hotel. I had been to a stretch of the Parkway once ten years earlier when I went to Charlottesville with my parents and we explored Monticello and Shenandoah National Park. Now I was going to go on a stretch of the Parkway I had never been on.

I left my hotel and drove down Highway 39 into Virginia past the point where I had made a wrong turn into that state on my previous trip. That part of the state with the Allegheny Mountains is basically a series of ridges and valleys that run parallel to each other in a north-northeast- south- southwest direction. Highway 39 went across these ridges constantly climbing one ridge and then descending the other side until it settled on a river valley that it followed out of the mountains. Soon I was on a broad hilly plain with tall mountains in the distance that had a blue haze- these were the Blue Ridge. This was an area filled with historic towns, including the Lexington that is home to the Virginia Military Institute. One thing I liked about that area was the warm weather that time of year. The temperature was in the 40s- a bit cold for what I was used to but about ten degrees warmer than 2000 feet in elevation farther up in Green Bank. This was something I liked about that area. I could easily drive to the lower places if I would get too cold in the winter, and if I got hot in the summer I could easily drive 2000 feet up in elevation to Snowshoe where it rarely gets above 75 degrees.

I entered the Parkway at the gap formed by the James River, a low spot along the road, but right after the river the road began winding up the mountain, finally cresting at about 3500 feet. I enjoyed the broad views from this solitary ridge that was far from the other mountains, but neither did I like being back in below freezing weather as I went up. I stayed on the Parkway until Roanoke, back at only 1000 feet elevation and beautiful weather if you discount the pollution in the cities, but I returned to my hotel right after.

My hotel was only five hours from Virginia Beach and I told myself if I drove all the way to West Virginia again I needed to drive all the way back to the Atlantic. As such, two days after doing the Blue Ridge Parkway I headed out for the coast. I headed back out on highway 39, but I did not want to continue on that slow highway to its end and instead shortcutted on a small road I found in my atlas at a point where that highway was close to I-64. This was indeed a very narrow road winding through the mountains, and as was unfortunately the case with many of these roads once the houses were passed, the pavement ended without warning. I was going to turn back around, but there was not an easy place to do that, and by looking at the position of the sun I was headed in the right direction. I stayed on the unpaved road for more than twenty minutes, passing nothing but forests and a couple bikers, until I finally got to a paved highway in a small hamlet called- what else- California. I looked at the sun and the shadows to try to decide which direction the freeway would be, and I decided to turn right. According to my map, the freeway would be right next to me. I turned right, drove for more than a mile, and there was still no sign of the freeway, so I decided I should have turned left. I made a U-turn, went past the unpaved road, and soon saw a sign saying Goshen was in 12 miles. That was back along highway 39, so I turned back around. When I got to the unpaved road, instead of going straight now, I turned left onto the continuation of that road, which was now paved. There were houses along it and the addresses were in the 800s and going down. Knowing how addresses work in some of these places, they would go down to zero in less than a mile and that would likely be another major junction. What happened was that the houses soon stopped and the pavement again ended, but soon the road went under a tall steel structure- that was the freeway. The only problem was that there was no onramp, but the road did continue on the other side of the freeway, paralleling it with the pavement resuming, and soon joined U.S. 60, which ran parallel to the Interstate at that point. The 60 turned out to be quite fast and I stayed on it through Lexington, this time passing its beautiful downtown going west-east instead of north-south.

My first stop was Appomattox, the place where Robert E. Lee surrendered on April 9th 1865 ending the Civil War. One of my friends from Manhattan Beach was born on April 9th and I told her that was the day the Civil War ended. I decided I needed to visit the place where it happened (all right, that was not the only reason why I was visiting Appomattox, but I was excited to be able to tell "Ashley Surrender" that I was there).

I drove into the town of Appomattox, got out in downtown, and thought to myself that that was where it happened. Except that was not where it happened. It happened at the site of the old Appomattox six miles to the east. I went on to that place.

That was a restored village of beautiful brick homes spaced a good distance from each other. No one lived there anymore- the new Appomattox was right along the railroad and by the late 19th century all the inhabitants of the old Appomattox had moved. The National Park Service now kept the old village as the landscape that appeared in newspaper photographs from when Lee surrendered.

I walked into the courthouse, knowing the surrender happened at Appomattox Court House. This was the Visitor Center and museum, but the whole inside was modern and looked nothing like a 19th century courthouse. I had some questions for the people there. First, why did the surrender happen in remote Appomattox of all places. Why not in Richmond, the Confederate capital, or Washington

D.C. I was told that it happened in Appomattox because there was a battle there, and when Lee saw that Union forces were closing in on him and that they would likely end up winning the war, he had no choice but to surrender. Secondly, why was the Courthouse not restored to its original appearance if that was where the surrender happened. I was told this was a common misconception. Not too much happened at the courthouse. The whole village was known as Appomattox Court House (a convention used in other counties in the mid-Atlantic where the county seat has the name of the county plus the "Court House" designation). The signing of the surrender documents happened at someone's house in the village.

I went into the gift shop located in a nearby restored house. Working there was a young girl who told me she was taking online classes at Dominion University. I asked her if Appomattox was a Native American name and she told me it was. Then I asked her something that I had thought since I was in sixth grade. Didn't she think "Appomattox" sounded like "Approximate". She told me that it is not known for sure what exactly was the original indigenous pronunciation, but it is now pronounced "Appomattox" I told her "No. I was saying that the name 'Appomattox' kind of sounds like the word 'Approximate'". She did not find it too amusing, but I finally accomplished my goal of telling someone at that site what I had thought since sixth grade that the name of the place sounds like.

I then went to the exact, not approximate, location where the surrender documents were signed. All right, it was technically only the approximate location- the inside of the house was only open for tours and there were no more tours that day. I did nevertheless stand on the front porch and looked inside at the room where the document was signed and was thinking to myself that was where it happened. That was where the War Between the States came to an end.

From the site where the Civil War ended, I went to the place where Anglo America began- Jamestown. I was in quite a hurry to get there, knowing these sites close at 5 PM or thereabouts this time of year and not knowing if I would be able to make it on time. I thought of making this a two day trip, but I did not want to cancel a night at my hotel either and I decided I could do the whole trip to the Atlantic and back on one day. As such, I did not drive through Richmond this time, I took the freeway around the city and would visit Richmond at night on my way back.

I arrived at the James River estuary at 4:40 PM with the sun low on the horizon. I crossed the river on a bridge, realizing I was back on the Atlantic seaboard. I just hoped I could make it to Jamestown by 5:00, or that it would still be open once I got there. Missing its opening by just a few minutes would be very unfortunate. The road leading to Jamestown was quite beautiful, passing by historic plantations. I wanted to visit at least one of them, but I did not have time. Also, I visited similar plantations when I went to New Orleans with my parents nearly twenty years earlier.

I arrived at the turnoff to Jamestown at 5:10. There was a row of cars driving out, but I was the only one driving in, likely indicating the place had just closed. I made it all the way to the entrance by 5:15 and unfortunately the site was closed. However, it did not just close either. It closed at 4:30 and I was happy I at least did not just miss being able to go there. I satisfied myself with parking by the water, looking at the trees going down to the water's edge, and toward the island on which the first permanent British settlement in America was founded in 1607.

I continued down the Colonial Parkway along the coast of the James River, aglow in the final moments before sunset. Virginia Beach and the nearest part of the open Atlantic were another fifty miles away. If I would make it there, I would not make it back to West Virginia until very late, so with that part of the James being an estuary of the Atlantic, I decided to end my trip there. I parked at a parking lot, walked down to the water's edge, dipped my feet in, and looked out across the water to the opposite shore. I did not put my hands in this time, as I was not sure how clean the water was. I was on an estuary of the Chesapeake Bay, which in turn is an estuary of the Atlantic Ocean, but I was nevertheless at sea level and at a point that gets some of the Atlantic's salty currents, so I decided I had made it back all the way across the country.

I was right next to Williamsburg, the town with the Colonial center and the living history. Since this was a functioning town, it would be open 24/7. I just hoped the Colonial part would still be open. I got into Williamsburg. Through construction closures I was directed to a place across from the College of William and Mary with Colonial looking buildings. I parked there and went out to the main street. This was a shopping street! One with boutiques, restaurants, and ice cream parlors- essentially a Manhattan Beach with colonial buildings. Had Colonial Williamsburg really become that commercialized?

I walked down the main street. Soon these modern shops ended and I had arrived in the actual Colonial Williamsburg (the part I had been to previously, I was soon informed, was only built in the 1930s in a replica of the Colonial style). The living history with the horse drawn carriages and people in character had ended for the day. The buildings had closed. The historic district, still closed to automobiles, was now the domain of locals going on their evening walks.

Nevertheless, there was still plenty to see. Houses beautifully restored or rebuilt, with their vegetable gardens outside. Stores with no words on their signs but with wooden pictures representing what they sell, looking like something out of *The Handmaid's Tale*. I looked inside one of the houses trying to see what of the living history that I could, and I found a flat screen TV and a remote control. Even in Colonial Williamsburg, some houses are modern tourist rentals or even private residences.

After walking several blocks down the streets of Colonial Williamsburg, I went back to the Colonial replica part and onto the campus of the College of William and Mary, the second oldest university in the United States after Harvard. When I went back to my car, I thought of going to Yorktown, the third site in the Colonial Triangle and the place where the final battle of the Revolutionary War was fought. However, it was already nighttime and I did not know how much I would see so I decided to head back. I headed out on Richmond Road, assuming this was at one time the main road to Richmond. I passed through more historic neighborhoods of Williamsburg before the road joined the modern U.S. 60 with its hotels and strip malls. Soon enough, I was back on the Interstate.

Now was my time to explore Richmond, the capital and largest city of Virginia. I got off the freeway at the edge of the Eastern neighborhoods and made it back to U.S. 60. Driving through these neighborhoods, I was wondering whether the city should be known as Poormond because it appeared quite run down. Downtown Richmond was nice, however, with its tall buildings, historic sites, and the theatre. West of downtown was a bit nicer than the eastside- I passed through a neighborhood of old brick apartments with the occasional brewery on the bottom floor. It was nothing like Portland, however. It still appeared quite inner city.

The road I was driving on soon ended at a shopping center, and right as I was turning onto the cross street, I found at that shopping center what I least expected- an organic, Whole Foods-like grocery store. I told myself I needed to go there for dinner, and I immediately turned into the shopping center. I frequently shopped and ate at these stores back home, but in West Virginia they were not to be found. The store was a bit smaller than the usual Whole Foods or Bristol Farms, but nevertheless did have a good selection. I got myself some Moroccan spiced chicken with no antibiotics or hormones and a side of fruit to liven up my bland, largely unhealthy, diet at the restaurants of the rest of my trip.

After the grocery store, I realized I was no longer in the poorer part of town. The houses were still of the historic brick type, but they were now elegant ones more worthy of the city's "rich" name. I re-entered the freeway in the suburbs, after getting a bit lost. Soon I passed through Charlottesville. I did not need to get off the freeway there, as I had already been there ten years earlier. West of Charlottesville is where the urbane East Coast ends and Appalachia begins. As relieved as I was to be going back to low EMF radiation country, I was also sad to leave the more sophisticated culture that I was used to behind. I arrived back at my hotel right after midnight. It was cold and I was the only guest there.

I was becoming more and more convinced that the area around Green Bank, West Virginia was the place for me, but there were some things I wanted to be sure about. I wanted to know where you could get organic groceries and grass fed beef there. If this was a place where people moved to escape harmful radiation, they would also want to avoid harmful chemicals in their foods and I wanted to know where in rural West Virginia you could get that food. The IGA store in Marlinton had only a very limited selection of organic fruits and no grass fed or antibiotic-free meats. For that matter, it had a very limited selection of anything that was good quality. I was told that a store in Green Bank did have some grass fed meats. When I went there, they did indeed have a good meat selection, but they did not know if any of them were grass fed. They told me all their meats came from other states and they did not know if they were grass fed or antibiotic free (if they are not labeled as such it usually means they are not). They told me to go to the other grocery store in Marlinton and that they likely had what I was looking for. I went to the store in Marlinton. It was the same story as the other store. They told me to go to the store in Green Bank, and I told them I was just there. Not having grass fed beef available in small towns and rural areas is nothing unusual, but there was something unusual here. All around Green Bank were pastures of grass grazing cows. Where was their meat being sold?

I went to the Kroger in Lewisburg and they did have a good selection of organic foods there, including meats, but again none of the meats were locally raised. Also, I would need to drive all the way to Lewisburg whenever I wanted to get organic or other good quality foods. A few days later, one of the electrosensitives told me she would get her food from a local wholesaler, but that you needed to make special arrangements with them and they were not available all the time.

When I was telling my parents I was ready to move to West Virginia, they told me they would fly down and we would pick a house for me. But that presented its own problems. I knew my parents would not do well in the cold and if they would experience the weather and the remoteness of that place they would be far less supportive of my move. I would need to go through a hellish week where I would be with my parents all the time and they would be very frustrated at me. Even if it would end with getting a house there, that experience with my parents would dampen any enjoyment I would have of that place.

It was understandable that my parents did not want me leaving them, so I suggested they move also. Maybe not to remote West Virginia, but somewhere in Virginia that was more urban and not too cold. Even if I did not move from California, I did not think that was a good place for them. They had no other family there besides my elderly uncle and uncle's wife. If something happened to my parents and my uncle and his wife would be dead or incapacitated, I did not know how much support I could give them. I was already struggling with his own life. My parents needed to be where they had more family. There was my cousin in Washington DC, my aunt and her children by Philadelphia, and if my parents would live somewhere near there and I would be not too far in West Virginia, they would have much more support than they would in Los Angeles. However, my parents were not ones to do that. My mother was open to that option, saying she would move near me if my father would die before her, but my father was not. He said that he was too old to move anywhere, especially somewhere that does not have the best weather.

There was another important issue for me, and that was a social life. When I asked an electrosensitive about that when she visited Casey at the hotel she told me that electrosensitives do not socialize much. I asked her if they do not just meet up with other electrosensitives. She told me not really, because most places where they can meet up have wi-fi. I asked her what about events at people's houses. She told me that that usually doesn't happen and that electrosensitives learn to be alone. I told her that that would be a problem for me, as I was someone in need of human interaction. She tried to convince me that it is good to be alone. Except I was alone already. I lived on my own. What I wanted was not to have to be alone all the time and to have an adequate amount of human interaction. I got into a huge argument with her about that matter, and she did not seem too sympathetic to my concerns. I told her that maybe because she was introverted she did not feel the same way I felt, but that electrosensitivity strikes extroverts also and we should not have to choose between exposure to harmful radiation and isolation. She said that maybe it did not seem that way, but she was actually an extrovert, and she was still able to learn to value her alone time.

I told her that all I wanted was people to get lunch with me, but she scoffed at the thought of that.

Then Casey's husband asked me if it was not enough that he and Casey had dinner with me. I told them that was good enough for me, but what would happen when the dog's owner would be back and Casey would not work at the hotel as much? Would they have dinner with me all the time once I would move into my house and no longer be a guest at the hotel? I reminded them that they were married and had their daughter so they did not need to socialize with everyone. I could not get married, so I needed the social company. Having Asperger's, marriage for me meant the C word- compromise on major things I would not change about myself. I reminded them of the five year old girl who stayed at the hotel with her dad the previous week and had dinner with us. Once she got her ice cream fix, she started talking loudly non stop. I went to the other room and only came back half an hour later when Casey called me to wash my plate. The girl was still being loud then. If I could not handle a child's noise for half an hour, I would not handle it for ten years. The guest responded that many people do not like noise, but once they have their own children they realize they love them so much that they no longer care about the noise. I told her that maybe that is true for people who were a little bothered by noise. I, however, REALLY did not like noise. Also, noise or no noise, I frankly do not like little kids too much and would not want to be around them 24/7 as a parent. Then she suggested that I find someone who does not want kids. I told her that most women who do not want to have children want to have dogs. Having to find someone who could live with an electrosensitive, marriage would indeed be very difficult for me and I did need to rely on a good amount of friends where I would only spend a limited amount of time with each.

The guest told me that finding a mate is indeed an issue for many electrosensitives, because so many people need cell phones and wi-fi. She told me that maybe I could make friends with the other electrosensitives without a mate who want to socialize. I was beginning to do that, but many of them were conspiracy theorists. Casey and her husband were not like that, but there were people there who believed the harm from cell phone radiation was intentional and one person told me it was a ploy by the government for mind control and to kill off a few million people. Even if I did not believe these things, those who did were both very convincing and frightening. The guest sympathized with me on that issue, acknowledging that it is not always healthy to be with people who are so pessimistic.

Casey and her husband now tried to help me with finding friends. The husband asked me if it mattered to me what age my friends were and I told him it didn't. He told me there was an old man working at the laundry who was very friendly. Then he told me about the librarian in Green Bank. I told him that I saw her there and she did not seem that social. He said that she is a very nice person and that the piano lady who used to work at the hotel was good friends with her. Then he asked me if I could handle being around wi-fi. I told him that I could for short periods of time- I was surrounded by it all the time in California. I just couldn't be right next to a router or people who were using their wireless devices. He told me that there were plenty of places with wi-fi where I could go and meet people, and that people who can handle a little wi-fi generally fare better socially, even around Green Bank.

As my stay wore on, I started getting tired of the food around Green Bank. There were a couple good places to eat, but I got tired of them fast. Many of the other places, however, were of the greasy spoon type. There were almost no options for spicy food there, even as that food had become popular nearly everywhere else in the country. I ended up going to Lewisburg more and more to eat at their fairly diverse selection of restaurants. One day I went back to the Chinese place. I was a bit hesitant to go there, as China was where the Coronavirus was coming from. However, I did not want to be racist against Chinese and also I asked myself what were the odds that Chinese restaurant operators in a small West Virginia town would have recently gone to Wuhan and brought back the virus.

When I was ready to have dinner that day, I went to the eclectic restaurant by my hotel, the one that was run by the son of the hotel's hippie-ish owners, but that was one of the days it was not open. I did not want to go all the way back to Lewisburg a second time, so I went to Marlinton. I got there at 8:30, but the restaurants that in October were open until 9 were now only open until 8, including the Dairy Queen. So if I did not want t satisfy myself with chips for dinner or risk having a dog try to nip me while heating up food in the kitchen, I again had to drive a long distance. I did not want to drive all the way back to Lewisburg, so I headed the other way toward Slatyfork and Snowshoe, hoping things would still be open when I got there. If not, I would need to go all the way to Elkins, a 70 mile drive from Marlinton. I got to Slatyfork and luckily there was a restaurant there open until 11. It was very much of a greasy spoon place, and there were some shady characters outside, but at least I got my hot dinner. I told myself that at least once I get my own house I could prepare my own food. I would still likely need to go to Lewisburg once a week for groceries, but other than that I would make food in my own kitchen that would be way better than any restaurant in Pocahontas County.

I followed Casey's husband's advice and went to talk with the librarian. She was a bit quiet and a bit country, like most people in that area were, but she did turn out to be very nice, and one whom I started visiting regularly. Then there was the store and restaurant of the Cass Railroad State Park. The people there also turned out to be friendly, especially the older woman who worked at the restaurant. The younger people there were a bit more reserved, but as I came there more and more they also started opening up. There was wi-fi in that building and the young people did go on their devices there, but not nearly as much as I saw them going on them in other places. What I liked was that the young people actually interacted with the old people, and did not hide on their screens like I have seen young people do in towns with an older leaning population. There were weekly events at that restaurant. On Friday there would be a trivia night and I told myself I would come to that to show them how good I am at trivia.

I decided now, with almost complete certainty, that this was the place I wanted to move to. I was sick of the place in California where people stood me up and where people were tied to their phones and dogs. In that place in West Virginia, if people told you they would meet up with you they would do that, at least that's what someone at the Cass restaurant told me. When I complained to her about how people in some places are not ashamed to say they like dogs more than people she told me that people do love their dogs in West Virginia also but that you need to like your human peers more. I had planned a hike with Jessica for Friday. My parents wanted me to come back to California already and sell my house without me wasting more money at the hotel before I move to my new house, but I told them that I wanted to stay at least until Friday to see if Jessica would honor her word and also see how the trivia would go.

Then that Wednesday, February 26th, it happened. I was at the library visiting my new friend when I went on the computers and saw there was a storm watch for Randolph County and the northwestern part of Pocahontas County. I was in the northeastern part of the county, but that did not mean the storm could not bring large amounts of snow or knock down the power lines. I decided I needed to get out that day.

I went back to my hotel to pack. I was quite hesitant to leave. The weather was beautiful that day, with the sun out and temperatures in the 50s. However, I could see the storm clouds moving in from the west and knew they would soon bring heavy rain which would turn in to snow as the temperatures would plummet. Back at the hotel, I looked up hotels in Charlottesville. It was in the opposite direction to California, but I could not head west, as that was where the storm was. Also, I had to go to Charlottesville regardless, as I needed a charger for my camera and that was the closest place to get one. At 4 PM I headed out for lunch when I ran by the hotel's horse stables into Jessica who was visiting her friend there. I told them that I was leaving because of the storm. The lady from the hotel told me "You can't leave. We need you here." I told her that I did not want to stay there if the lights might go off. She told me they had a generator and that it keeps the refrigerators and the heaters on. I asked her if it also keeps all the lights on and she told me it does.

I went back to the Cass Railroad building to see my friends there. I told them that I was thinking of heading out to Charlottesville. I really did not know what to do now. The people at the hotel really wanted me to stay and I was told the generator would keep the lights on in a blackout, but the person who told me that was not the owner and I was not sure if she knew. I was also feeling a bit sick that day and decided I might want some tea that night, but the teas and the brewer were right where the dog could get me. As such, with the storm clouds moving ever closer, I drove back to my hotel to pack. I tried calling the front desk four times but there was no answer. I wanted to make sure I would get a refund for the four nights I paid for that I would not be staying.

Then I called my parents telling them I was leaving my hotel but wanted to move to West Virginia. My dad again was not being supportive and started threatening me that I would be homeless if I would move there but then decide I would not want to stay. I told my mom now that I did not want to come back to California at all. I knew if I would come back it would be the same story as the previous time and all the previous trips I had made to look for a place to move to. My parents would not be supportive of my move and I would be back stuck in a place where I had all of my issues.

I finished packing right after the sun went down. I stood outside my hotel in the still nice weather, finding it hard to believe in this calm that a storm would soon be arriving. I stopped at the eclectic restaurant to see if anyone from the hotel was there. The owner was there and I asked her about the generators. Sure enough she told me they only powered the refrigerators and the heaters, but not the lights. I told her that I was leaving, and she understood I might not want to be there during a storm. I told her I might come back once the storm was over depending on what the weather would be like, and asked her if I would get a refund for the nights I would not be staying there. She told me that I could, and I headed out on the road now.

XI.   East, then West

It had started raining once I hit the road, with the rain soon growing heavy. But because I was headed east, I was able to outrun the storm and soon found myself out of the rain. The highway soon turned north right over the Virginia border and soon I was back in the storm, but was able to outrun it once the highway turned east. Then I was on U.S. 220, which ran north-south. It would be another eight miles to the east-west U.S. 250 and I hoped I could stay ahead of the storm until I got to that highway. Soon, however, I saw blue and red lights turning at me and sounding their siren. I knew I was speeding a little and told the cop that I was trying to get out before the storm. I hoped he would be sympathetic with his calm demeanor, but he was not. He held me up for over ten minutes, longer than I had ever been held up in a traffic stop before, and it soon again started to rain. Once I was on the 250, I did have some heavy rain and even lightning strike not too far from the road. In my citation appeal I put down that by citing me for going a few miles per hour over the speed limit, he delayed my drive to a time when the weather was more dangerous and thus put me at a greater danger to myself and others than what I was in by driving a few miles per hour over the speed limit. I did not win the appeal, thanks to a system that values "by the book" statutes more than actual risk.

I made it to Charlottesville despite the rain. I was happy to be back in a liberal and urbane college town, and once I saw a Tibetan restaurant I had to stop there for dinner. The food was good, but what that I did not like about that place was that they played a recording of traditional mantras where the same six syllable line was repeated about 200 times, interrupted only by musical breaks. If you are a practitioner of an Eastern religion or meditation regime you might want to hear and recite this, but if you are just coming to a restaurant to have thukpa stew or momo dumplings, these phrases repeated over and over again can drive you crazy. I was happy when the recording ended. This was followed by one with more upbeat music, but I soon realized it was another six syllable mantra repeated over and over. I quickly paid the bill after I finished eating and left.

There were two hotels that interested me in C-ville. The first was a bed and breakfast right next to the university. The building reminded me of some of the 1930s-era apartment buildings by UCLA, and the neighborhood, with its tree lined streets, reminded me of the neighborhood by that university where my uncle lived. I walked into the hotel, but did not see anyone inside. Then I asked myself why was I even trying to stay over there when there was a high rise full service hotel that went for about the same price. I went to the other hotel, got a room on the seventh floor, made myself decaffeinated tea without having to worry about a dog nipping me, and then went to sleep.

I told my mom she should move to Charlottesville. It was a cultural center with a good sized Jewish population, as my mother wanted, and only two hours from Green Bank. I would come out to Charlottesville whenever I wanted some culture and my mother could teach Hebrew at the University of Virginia. But my dad would never move to the unpleasant weather of Virginia, and my mother asked me wasn't Charlottesville the place with the white supremacist protests in 2017. The latter was indeed a concern of mine, but upon visiting C-Ville I found it to be the most liberal place in the whole region. If neo-Nazi marches could happen there, what could happen in West Virginia, one might ask. And if the white supremacist agitators in Charlottesville were not from there, and I am sure many of them were not, where were they from? That was why when my parents told their Jewish friends in L.A. that I wanted to move to West Virginia they told them that they should not let me. I told my parents that these people had probably never been to West Virginia and were just stereotyping its inhabitants. The formerly urban electrosensitives were not white supremacists. The friends I made at the restaurants told me they did not believe in racism and did not care much about politics. I am sure there are some white supremacists and anti-Semites there, but they generally don't do anything if they are not provoked. In Charlottesville, there were anti-racists protesting against them, and unfortunately, often when less kind people are told my others that they cannot do what they are doing, they turn violent. This is not to say, however, that the anti-racists were not justified in their fight.

The storm had passed and I was thinking of returning to Green Bank that day, but I was still very sick and it would not be good for me to go back up to the mountains with the temperature there still in the 20s. Snow was in the forecast for the following day, so a hike would not have been a good idea. As such, I continued to my next destination. I was too sick to travel far, so I only went another two hours southwest to Roanoke. It was at a lower elevation than Green Bank and still close enough to that place should the weather become warmer and I would feel well enough to return. Being sick, I could not do all the sightseeing I wanted, and having to socially distance also meant I could not talk to the people in the stores to see what the people are like in these places. I am not sure whether I had the Coronavirus, though I did experience some of its symptoms-fever, sore throat, difficulty breathing, and fatigue. That might be a reason why after that trip I never got the virus, at least not to my knowledge and not as of this writing. However, there would be no reported case of the virus in West

Virginia for a whole three weeks after I left there and none in Pocahontas County for more than two months, so most likely it was not Covid-19. What it might have been was one of the other four coronaviruses, which produce similar effects and immunity as Covid-19 but are far less dangerous.

I checked in to the Hotel Roanoke when I got into town. Built in 1882 in the style of a large European castle, this is one of the classic grand hotels in the United States, and being in Roanoke it was not too expensive. I got a room on the fifth floor with a view from a hill of the downtown buildings. I walked on the covered bridge across the railroad tracks into downtown and their marketplace to get lunch, dodging people walking by with their cell phones while I tried ordering my food. After lunch, feeling fatigued both from my illness and lack of sleep the previous night, I got back in my room and crashed in bed.

I woke up two hours later. I called Hailey to tell her happy birthday. She had invited me to her dinner and I planned to leave for the trip early enough to make it back by her birthday, but my parents kept telling me not to go until the spring and I told myself I would wait at least until after the birthday. Then when Monica stood me up for dinner I decided I could not take it anymore. It was probably a good thing I went when I did, as a month later the pandemic would start.

When I woke up it was 8 PM and cold outside. I still had not brought in my suitcase and I needed it for the night. I tried to find an exit closest to the parking lot so that I would not need to walk far in the cold. Unfortunately, that exit was a floor above the parking lot and I would not be able to roll my suitcase up the steps. I found an employee entrance at the same level as the parking lot and proceeded to go in there after taking my suitcase. Right as I was preparing to go in, two people came out on their break and one of them was getting ready to light his cigarette right at the doorway. I told him "Don't smoke in front of me!" When he would not listen, I told him that again and he finally put away his lighter.

I had forgotten to take my sodas with me and an hour later had gotten very thirsty from all the liquids I lost through sneezing. As such, I went down to the lobby to use the vending machine. It did not take cards so I had to withdraw money from the ATM. The machine would not take my card, however, so I went to look for other ATMs and vending machines, but there were none that I found. I asked at the reception and they told me that was all they had. I did not want to go back out in the cold to get my drinks when I was sick, so I asked the receptionist if he could get me something from the vending machines and have it charged to my room. He told me he wasn't authorized to do that. I told him that it was an emergency and I could not go back to my car. He said that he could ask his manager. He went to do that, but the manager said no. Again I told him it was an emergency. I asked myself what type of four star hotel was this where they would make me go back to my car in the cold to get a soft drink. Finally he told me I could get a drink at the bar.

I went to the bar, also to get dinner, but it was not a socially distanced environment, so I decided to order room service. I called and asked for two Sprites to be delivered with my food, which I soon changed to three Sprites. Normally I do not order room service or even eat in the hotel restaurants, as that is expensive, but under these circumstances I was willing to have things a bit more expensive if it meant not getting more sick. When the butler brought my food up and the $10.50 worth of Sprite, he told me I had a great view from my room. I gobbled down a whole 20 ounce bottle of Sprite with my hamburger and fries and got nearly through the second one, being that dehydrated.

The following day it was still too cold in Green Bank and I was still sick, so I e-mailed Jessica telling her I could not go on the hike. Jessica did not have any type of phone whatsoever- she was also sensitive to landlines- but she did regularly check e-mails at the library. Then I looked for places to stay a couple hours west of Roanoke, as I was still too sick to travel farther, and I made a reservation for a place in Kingsport, Tennessee.

I started driving up the continuation of the Blue Ridge Parkway from where I was before, as it was on my way to Kingsport, but the temperature quickly dropped into the 30s as I went up the mountains and the drive was very slow. I decided this was best left for when I was feeling better and soon turned off the parkway to join the Interstate. I could not escape the cold for long, however. I still had to go through the mountain passes and the temperature did drop later in the day. But I was also in my heated car and did not need to get out of it for much. When I got over the Tennessee border it started snowing, a snow that alternated with heavy rain and then back into snow.

I again took a long nap at my hotel, waking up at 8 PM to walk around. I was going to go to their restaurant to eat (it was still too cold and I was still too sick to go out), but the place crowded. The whole hotel was very crowded, full of people there for a high school volleyball convention. As such, I again ordered room service.

The following morning I left my hotel at 9 AM without having breakfast. I was feeling a bit better, so I could handle a longer drive. I decided to drive out to Lexington, Kentucky, a six hour drive (or five without stopping). I did not make any reservations, as Lexington was a large place with many hotel options and I was still not completely recovered so I was not sure I could handle driving all the way to Lexington.

I headed north on U.S. 23 back across the Virginia border and then west on U.S. 58 to the Cumberland Gap. This was still the state of Virginia, but it did not feel like it. This was the extreme western part of the panhandle and extended farther west than the westernmost point of West Virginia. Even the landscape and the community design here looked very western- it looked more like what I saw in New Mexico or Colorado than that of an east coast state. This was the country through which Daniel Boone led hunting packs, and there were places named for him all over that area. This was where country music as we know it originated. This was the Wilderness Road along which the first white settlers to the areas west of the Appalachians traveled. This was the first American frontier.

First American frontier is a bit subjective. Before that area was settled, Charlottesville was the frontier. Before Charlottesville was settled, Jamestown was the first Anglo American frontier, or it was the ill fated Roanoke Colony in North Carolina if you want to include that. Alaska was the first American frontier for any human settlement when the ancestors of the Native Americans crossed the landbridge, and Alaska is still the last U.S. frontier per its state's motto. However, there is a difference here. This part of Virginia, Tennessee, and Kentucky was the frontier at the time of the American Revolution and right after. The settlements here were not established by the British but by Americans. These settlements were not established to enrich a royal crown or even much for the sake of enriching any government, but were established by and for the people. These were places established by people who wanted adventure, their own land, and to escape the trappings of society so that they could have more freedom. This was where the notion of the American frontier was born, a frontier that kept moving farther west until all of the country became settled. This was where the concept of rugged individualism was born.

I continued toward the Cumberland Gap, the path of least resistance through the mountains that the Wilderness Road took. I had wanted to visit that place since first learning about it in my high school U.S. history class. The mileposts on Highway 58 were counting toward the gap and I could not wait to actually go through there. Right after milepost 2, there was a sign for Cumberland Gap National Historic Park and a turn into the park. I figured that was the old road through the gap instead of the four lane expressway I was heading on, but I missed the turn. I tried to turn back around, but could not do that until I reached milepost zero and was back over the Tennessee border. I made a U-turn there, heading back into Virginia, and this time turned at the park's entrance. That road dead ended at a parking lot with hiking trails, including one that went along the old footpath. It was too cold for a hike, so I turned back around, back onto the expressway and back to Tennessee.

At the same place where I made the first U-turn I now made a right turn to the town of Cumberland Gap. I thought this would be where the old road across the gap would pass and I did not want to take the very un-historic freeway tunnel across this pass. The right turn put me back over the border in Virginia, but only for about a thousand feet before turning back south into Tennessee. I stopped in the town of Cumberland Gap- small and historic but quite lively, in large part due to it being two miles from LMU. I saw a sign for the LMU university in Knoxville and I found it very weird. It was the initials of my university, Loyola Marymount University, except here it was not. In Cumberland Gap, LMU signs were found all over the place and I stopped by a boutique with such a sign and had a chat with the old lady there. She told me the LMU here stood for Lincoln Memorial University and that they would get many people from there in Cumberland Gap. I also got into a conversation with her about smartphones and she also did not like how many young people, including her own children, were constantly on their devices.

I was trying to look for the old road across the gap, but found myself going in a circle back to the modern expressway. I had no choice but to go through (more correctly right next to) the Cumberland Gap by the tunnel. This time, I crossed into Kentucky- I had passed the western most point of Virginia. Later on I found out that the automobile road though the gap no longer existed. Once the tunnel and expressway were completed in the 1990s the old highways were turned back into hiking trails to restore their frontier days appearance.

An hour after the un-historic tunnel, I arrived in the town of Corbin. It was nearly 1 PM and I still had not had breakfast and I tried finding a place to eat. Downtown had a couple restaurants, but they were not too appealing. Then just north of downtown, I passed by a KFC that was connected to a historic building. Was this the original Kentucky Fried Chicken? I stopped to look around. Indeed it was. This was where Colonel Sanders opened a gas station in 1932 for travelers along what was then the main highway from Michigan to Florida, and right where the western and eastern branches of U.S. 25 split up (the split has moved a few miles north since then). In 1940, he expanded to include a motel and his fried chicken restaurant. The ordering counter at this location was in a glass brick modern building, but the eating area was in the 1940 building, beautifully restored with its dark wood panelings and tables. There was a display of Colonel Sanders's original kitchen where he perfected the art of frying chicken in a pressure cooker for travelers who wanted their meals fast. There was also a model of the motel rooms, something he had in his original restaurants so that travelers wanting to stay there could see what the rooms were like before booking one (this would be a great concept to have in modern hotels, especially for people who don't make reservations). When the Interstate Highway Act was signed in 1956, Colonel Sanders knew it would be just a matter of time before his restaurant would be bypassed by a freeway and the customers would disappear. As such, he expanded his restaurant to open franchises the world over. As I have already stated, I am not a huge fan of KFC, but this was the original one so how could I resist eating there. I stood there debating for a long time whether I should eat there. Finally I decided that I was still sick and I did not want to have Kentucky fried antibiotic laced fast food chicken, so I went on. I got gas at the gas station where the colonel's motel used to stand and then I went on. I ended up eating at another fast food place- there were not too many options in small town Kentucky- but at least there they had a fish sandwich, which is a bit healthier than fast food chicken.

I got into Lexington at around 3:30. I went to the Residence Inn at the Southern part of town, but they did not have a room. I was thinking of staying at the Marriott resort, but it was a bit expensive. Then I went to another Residence Inn closer to downtown, but it was right next to a cell tower and the freeway so I did not want it. I ended up staying at the Embassy Suites across from the Marriott resort. I took a long nap, got up two hours later to have my Chobani yogurt, and just hung around my hotel. Just after 9 PM, I left to go have dinner, being the time restaurants would clear up that Saturday night. Some places I wanted to go to were closed, others were packed. I ended up going to P.F. Chang's at 10 PM, a favorite Chinese place of mine except for it being a bit too Americanized, and there was hardly a soul there.

XII. The River Cities

After heading out of Lexington the following morning, I got off the freeway in Frankfort to see Kentucky's capital. I then took U.S. 60 for some distance and was going to get back on the freeway, but the old highway was fairly fast and I stayed on it for the whole sixty mile drive to Louisville. I stopped for lunch at a trendy Greek eatery in midtown. I tried to go into the boutiques, but this was a place where not too many places were open on Sunday. Still, overall, Louisville seemed like a very livable city. It was not too large, not too small. It had charming historic neighborhoods with nice coffeeshops and boutiques. The town also seemed racially integrated.

Twelve days after my visit to Louisville, an incident happened there that made me change some of my perceptions about that place. That was when police broke into the apartment on a knockless warrant where black Breonna Taylor was living and, following an armed confrontation between the police and her boyfriend, fired multiple shots and killed her. Had the residents of the apartment been white, the police would have most likely not reacted with that level of force and Breonna Taylor would still be alive. Then two months later, George Floyd was killed by police in Minneapolis, a city that I had long thought to be one of the most friendly and tolerant in the United States. There are two possible explanations for this. One is that these were isolated incidents that do not represent most of the citizenry of these cities. Another is that these places are not as tolerant as they make themselves out to be. In Minneapolis we know there were several other incidences of police using excessive force on blacks and even killing them. These places are friendly, tolerant, and like diversity, but only to an extent. They like different ethnic foods. They like different ethnicities of white. They also like Hispanics, Asians, and even many blacks. However, they only truly like the blacks that are well behaved. If they are criminals, or even if they are poor, the rest of the population does not want to integrate with them, and those in charge will deal harshly with them when they do something out of line. As I had seen on my drives down the old surface highways through the cities, these cities had the nicer neighborhoods of mostly whites with some nonwhites to "integrate" the place, but elsewhere in town, poor black or Mexican ghettos, run down as ever, still existed. That was the case in Louisville along Muhammad Ali Boulevard west of downtown.

After Louisville, I crossed the Ohio River into Indiana. I was now back in the Midwest and north of the Mason-Dixon Line. I was headed to Evansville where I planned on spending the night, but again had not made reservations. I also wanted to go to the town of Santa Claus whose name I long found to be bizarre and which was now on my way. Getting off the freeway for that place, and taking a few miles of the scenic route, I found myself in the town of St. Meinrad. The next thing I knew was that on a hill above town there stood a monastery of a Gothic construction. These are commonly found in Europe but I did not expect to find one in rural Indiana! I drove onto the grounds, went into the gift shop down the hill, and asked the saleswoman questions about that place. She told me there would be a tour and a performance of their choir at 5 PM if I wanted to stick around, and that I was free to walk around the grounds. All of this was tempting, but I did not have time- not if I wanted to make it to my hotel before the sun was low. I took one more brief look and drive past the abbey before continuing on.

Santa Claus, Indiana did not have much going for it except for the name. Even though its official population is 2400, it does not appear nearly that large. The only evident signs of the town were a couple houses along Highway 245, signs saying "Welcome to Santa Claus, Indiana", and the Holiday World theme park that was closed for the season.

I still had another forty miles to Evansville and I was not sure if I could get there before the sun would be low. The sky was overcast, but farther west there was an opening in the clouds from which the sun would come out, so I looked to see if there were any places closer to Evansville or in another direction and where there would likely be good quality hotels. I found the town of Owensboro 30 miles to the south and back across the river in Kentucky. I headed there now. I took Highway 231 past another radiation emitting structure, albeit a different type of radiation than the microwaves of cell phones, a nuclear power plant. Then I was over a new bridge over the Ohio River and back in Kentucky. I turned off the 231 for Owensboro, passing through a very run down industrial area that made me ask if I really wanted to stay in that town. Then I got to their downtown, which was quite nice. Past downtown and along the river was where I found the hotels. There was a newish multi-story Hampton Inn, not where I wanted to stay. The next hotel was a Holiday Inn, and there were none after.

The Holiday Inn was the nicer of the two, but still not a brand that seemed very good. I walked inside, asked the receptionist if there were any other hotels in town. She told me to go down another street and I would find a Motel 6 and a Super 8 there. I asked her if there were any Hiltons or Marriotts in town, and she told me there were not. The Holiday Inn was the nicest hotel in town and I got a room there. And this was actually a nice hotel, especially with the river view.

Owensboro is one of those towns known for its barbecue, and I was determined to go to one of its landmark eateries. I went to one of them, but it was closed, this being a "Never on Sunday" Bible Belt area. I went back to my hotel looking to see where the other landmark eatery was, then went straight back out, hoping to get there before the 8 PM closing time. That eatery was in the middle of the industrial area, and I could not even find it. I went back to downtown. It was after 8 PM now and I walked into the only eatery I saw open. I asked one of the workers if there were any barbecue places that were open at that time. He told me that all those places would be closed at that time, but told me I could try another landmark place on the southern end of town. I went there, and they were fortunately open until 9. Owensboro's specialty is lamb barbecue. I regularly make lamb kabob and grilled lamb chops at my house, so it was an interesting experience having Southern barbecue with lamb. Definitely try it if you are ever in Owensboro.

Owensboro is just south of the Ohio River, the border with Indiana, and the demarcation line between North and South. I asked one of the waitresses if there was a major cultural difference between Owensboro and the places immediately north in Indiana even though they were only a few miles away and she told me there was.

I went to sleep at ten that night and woke up right after five in the morning. I was going to continue sleeping, but I decided, as I did in Phoenix on my previous trip, that I had accumulated enough sleep that night and in my previous day's nap to get up now and take advantage of the early time. I drove over the bridge from downtown Owensboro into Indiana as dawn was breaking. Soon I was on highways through the farm country driving with commuters whose day began early. I was a bit bothered by the headlights, but as soon as I approached Evansville the road became a four lane expressway.

Soon the road went back down to two lanes. Even though the sun was up by now, it was raining, so the oncoming cars still had their lights on. There were now many more cars than before, so I had to get off that road. I turned onto a small farm road with no traffic. The road headed north toward the Interstate, but a mile later that road ended at someone's barn and another road turned due east. I took that road, even though it was in the opposite direction, and a mile later I turned onto a road going north. That road ended at a T intersection a couple miles later and I now turned west. That road, through a couple of turns through a wooded area, led me back to the highway I was on before with its multitude of oncoming cars. I immediately turned off that road, but this time to a state highway going north. It was not without traffic, but did have significantly less traffic than the previous highway and I was soon on the wide Interstate.

By ten I had made it to the suburbs of St. Louis. My first stop was the Cahokia Mounds. I had first learned about them in that sixth grade history class where I learned about the Carlsbad Caverns. They were built nearly a thousand years ago by a Native American tribe to serve as ceremonial structures for a town that likely had 30 000 residents at its peak. Now the mounds were situated among a huge park surrounded by suburban development. I made my way to the largest mound, over a hundred feet tall, built on multiple levels, and fourteen acres in size. I climbed up the stairs to the top. The climb was exhausting, all the more so because of the cold and the fact that I was still sick, but I made it all the way to the top, from where for the first time I saw the skyline of St. Louis with its Gateway Arch. I ran into a local who was running up the mound and back down several times, and he told me that was his daily exercise.

Out of all the new places I visited on my second trip, St. Louis was probably the one I was most excited about. When I was growing up, my father went on business trips there all the time. Working for Northrop Aircraft, he would go there every couple months for meetings with McDonnell Douglas (now part of Boeing), a company Northrop regularly worked with and that had large plants both in Southern California and St. Louis. As such, St. Louis was practically his second home, and St. Louis for me was synonymous with my dad going away for some time. I always tried to imagine at that time what St. Louis was like. What were the street addresses like? What did the neighborhoods look like? By in large, I had imagined it looking like places in Los Angeles. Many people when they hear of unfamiliar places think of them as looking like the places that they know.

My dad stopped going to St. Louis when I was thirteen. With the promotions he got and a more global economy, he now went to places like Europe or South Korea. My dad never liked St. Louis too much, but as I got older and learned more about the city's sites and history, I was the one who wanted to go. Once when a college friend of mine was thinking of going to nursing school there I was thinking of going with my dad to visit, but that friend never ended up going there. Now on this road trip I finally had the opportunity to go to St. Louis.

I made it over one of the bridges over the Mississippi into Downtown St. Louis and told myself this was St. Louis. This was the city my dad went to all the time when I was growing up. Even though I heard from the media that St. Louis was a very run down place, downtown actually looked quite nice, with fancy office buildings, well kept historic highrises, and upscale hotels. My first stop was the Gateway Arch. The arch represents the gateway to the West, and to me that meant I would soon be back to my parents who were not supportive of my move. Again I asked myself if I should just turn around now and go back to West Virginia.

I did not think much of going back to West Virginia now. I wanted to focus on seeing the sites. The 630 foot tall arch is quite impressive when you see it up close and study its architecture- the triangle shaped tube that climbs and spreads out in the form of an arch and that is clad in stainless aluminum, forming a symbol of the city known the world over. Complementing this 1960s arch design is a gallery underneath the park in front of the arch. That International Style space is vast and resembles an airport terminal, in sharp contrast to the American history exhibits depicted inside the building.

I have two problems with the Gateway Arch complex. One is all the historic buildings that had to be cleared to build the arch. Yes, by the 1930s (when planning of the monument first began) that neighborhood was quite run down. But it was also where St. Louis got started, and we will now never have that neighborhood again. Had it been saved, it could have become today a vibrant draw for both tourists and locals just like the colonial part of Philadelphia or the French Quarter of New Orleans are now. Instead, that old quarter is now only depicted in dioramas inside the museum that tells the story of the central role St. Louis played as the jumping off point for Western expansion.

Another issue is that the Trump Administration had recently declared it a National Park. Yes, the Gateway Arch is an American landmark, but it is also human made. A National Park is supposed to be for natural places. Human made structures should be designated as National Monument (as it had been previously designated) or National Historic Site. To me this was an example of the Trump Administration adding a National Park but also watering down its ideal, a practice done by an administration that did not care much about the natural environment and that shrank the sizes of other national monuments. When I presented that argument to the person who took my ticket, he did not agree with me. He said that because of what it represents that place was worthy of the prestigious title of "National Park". Maybe he was right. This country is built of dramatic natural places as well as human made ones. And both are worth preserving and celebrating.

When I was in high school, one of my Midwestern teachers gave me a book on the architecture of St. Louis. I saw in that book that you can actually ride to the top of the arch and see the view from there. When I asked my teacher about it, she told me she had never done it but heard that it gets very claustrophobic on the ride up. I told myself if I would ever go to the top of the arch I would go early in the morning on a weekday when there would be very few people. Now I asked the person who took my ticket about that and he told me that some people get claustrophobic but others do not. He pointed me to an actual size model of the tram, as it is known. It had five seats and they were tiny. It was not particularly crowded that day and I was not sure that all five seats would be filled. In pre-smartphone days, I would have likely bit the bullet and gone to the top, but now I decided to skip that.

Heading west from downtown, I made a quick stop at the Union Station, hearing this was a well designed urban renewal project with a hotel and shops. I went inside, but only stayed a few minutes because there was a crowded convention. I soon found myself driving through some of the nice historic neighborhoods around Forest Park, and then drove into the park, site of the 1904 World's Fair.

The 1904 World's Fair was quite a landmark one. It coincided with the Olympics held in St. Louis when that was the fourth largest city in the U.S. and one of the thirty largest in the world. Today the city proper is dying and only has one half the population it had at that time. While the metropolitan area is still at a good size of nearly three million, it no longer is in the top twenty of the United States. It was at that fair where the American hot dog was invented as well as the ice cream cone. A Lebanese immigrant making flatbread decided to buy ice cream from the stand next to him and put scoops of it on top of his rolled up flatbread, thus giving birth to a new American food. The story goes that the ice cream place ran out of bowls and that was when the flatbread maker decided to use that to hold the ice cream. Forest Park still has remnants of that World's Fair with its beautifully landscaped grounds, including a large pool with fountains that looked like something from Versailles.

I was not sure where I was going to spend that night, but after Forest Park I decided I was too tired to continue past St. Louis. I used my travel logic to figure out where the hotels would be, and I did not want to backtrack to downtown. I went to University City, an upscale suburb and college town just west of the city limits. The place had tree lined streets with nice old brick homes, office buildings, and boutiques I would have hung out at had I lived there, but I did not find any hotels. I made my way to I-170, knowing hotels are often located by freeway exits. I drove there for a couple exits. I did not find any Hiltons or Marriotts, but I did find a Drury Inn. I got off the freeway, went into the hotel to ask if they had vacancies, and they did. But then I decided I did not know too much about this chain and it did not seem like it was a better one so I continued on.

I decided there would be a wide selection of hotels by the airport. This was my dad's entry place into St. Louis, and he probably stayed at the hotels by the airport sometimes. Plus, he worked in aerospace, so staying by the airport in St. Louis was very appropriate for me. When I was right next to the airport, I saw a Renaissance Hotel on the other side of the freeway. I exited, but the road planners did not make it easy to get to the other side. There were turns for the airport terminals and car rental spaces, but none to get across the freeway. I ended up driving about two miles through crowded airport rush hour traffic until I was finally able to get across the freeway. By that time, I passed a Hilton and a Marriott. I still decided the Renaissance was better so I head back over there. I got to the Renaissance- no cell phone receptors on the roof. There was a cell tower nearby, but it was far enough from the hotel. I went inside- the lobby was crowded and there was a long wait, and being by the airport cell phone use there was heavy, so I left. I went back to the Marriott, but its roof was cell receptors galore, so that left me with the Hilton.

I did not see any cell receptors on the Hilton's roof or any cell tower nearby. After turning into the hotel, however, I noticed that the rods on the top of the billboard in front of the hotel had three cell receptors on them. They were small, and the hotel's towers were quite far from the billboard, so I decided to stay there. I parked my car, went into the lobby, and booked a room. However, soon after booking my room, I started getting a headache. I went up to my room. When I got out on the seventh floor, I now saw that on the clerestory of a one story part of the hotel there were a couple of cell receptors- placed unusually low- and pointing toward the hotel! My room was way down the corridor and the receptors were at the way other end of the large hotel, so maybe I would be fine. However, I still went back down to the lobby to look at other hotels. I saw downtown had a couple of nice hotels that were actually cheaper than that Hilton. I went back to the front desk and asked the receptionists if I would be able to cancel my reservation. They asked me why did I want to do that and I told them I found a better deal somewhere else. Then they canceled my reservation. I went back on the computer to research the hotels more. I decided that the downtown hotels would probably charge more for parking, thus raising the price to about that of the Hilton. Also, cell receptors are found everywhere in downtowns, I did not want to drive back there in rush hour traffic, and I was already at the hotel by the airport, so I told the receptionists I would like to keep my reservation.

Twenty minutes later, I left my hotel for a late lunch. Exiting the parking lot, I noticed that that raised one story portion had more cell receptors than I thought. The front part had a whole array of them, at a well trafficked Hertz Rental place that was connected to the hotel and only ten feet above the ground! I now for sure wanted to leave that hotel. I would just find a place to have lunch and then go back to check out. But there were no places for lunch around my hotel. Behind the row of airport hotels was one of the many run down neighborhoods of St. Louis. I went back to the hotel without having lunch and told the receptionists that I hoped it was still not too late to cancel. They told me that it was actually a bit too late, so I stayed, despite the cell receptors. I got lunch at the hotel's slightly expensive restaurant.

One of my concerns about wireless radiation is pathogens being able to enter the brain when someone is sick. Still not being 100 percent well, I was highly concerned about this during my stay. Studies, however inconclusive, show that wireless radiation can damage the blood-brain barrier, thus enabling toxins to more easily enter the brain and cause damage. We now see that Covid-19 causes long term neurological damage in some people, more so than other viruses do. I do not believe the conspiracies that Covid is caused by 5G. Viruses and radiation are two completely different things and 5G is not necessarily worse than 4G or 3G. However, that is not to say wireless radiation does not affect the brain and cannot contribute to the neurological damage suffered by people who have a disease. If that is indeed the case, especially with Covid, it is very troubling.

The hotel had a fairly good amount of negative online reviews, mostly concerned how dated the property looked. Indeed, everything from the exterior to the décor in the rooms looked very late 70s/ early 80s. I, however, liked this. It gave the hotel a unique retro look that reminded me of my childhood and was reminiscent of the times my father went to St. Louis. I also wondered if he had ever stayed at that hotel. I thought overall it was a good hotel except for the cell receptors and heavy wireless use on the property.

For dinner, I decided to go to St. Charles, the historic town on the Missouri River that was now a suburb of St. Louis only eight miles from my hotel. Driving across the river, a 25 story casino was looming in front of me and I asked myself why did I not stay there. I made it to the historic center of St. Charles. Being on the Missouri River only a few miles west of its junction with the Mississippi, this was at one time considered the last "civilized" Anglo town before the frontier. With its cobblestone streets and brick balconied buildings, it looked like the popularly imagined landscape of Tom Sawyer or, as was the case with so many other places I saw on my trips, like parts of Disneyland. This looked like a cross between Main Street USA (which was based on a town in Missouri) and Frontierland. When I was a child, my dad on one of his trips got my mom a teal blue T-shirt of a riverboat called "The Spirit of St. Charles", a shirt that for a couple years my mother wore all the time. I associated the shirt with where I knew the name St. Charles from- a street in Monopoly- and found it quite interesting it appeared on my mom's shirt.

I tried to find a place to eat, but due to my late lunch I was not hungry enough to eat dinner until 9:00 and once I got to the historic part of St. Charles the restaurants were closed. I made my way down the expressway along the river and found a Waffle House that was open late. I had never eaten at a Waffle House before and decided to check it out. However, once I looked at the menu, I saw that it was all starchy food. I had a lot of it that day and wanted something more healthy now. There were no other nearby restaurants in that industrial area, so I got on the freeway and got off at the next exit looking for places. I found an Italian restaurant that was still open. My dad told me about how he went a couple times in St. Louis to these steakhouses that served two pound steaks that people could not finish, and with sharing not being allowed, they took the remaining part of their steak home. I wanted to go to one of these good steakhouses, but not knowing where I would find one that was still open, I went to the so-so Italian place.

Back at my hotel, I e-mailed my dad. I told him that we had switched places. Now instead of he being in St. Louis and contacting me in Los Angeles, I was the one there and contacting him at home. I told him about all the places I visited and asked him if he had even been to them. He responded with a summary of the work he did in St. Louis. He also said that he was familiar with all the places I told him about, but that in all his years there he had never been to them or any other tourist spot. He was always very busy with work and meetings. He told me of one time where he had meetings all day and all the following night, and the following morning he had another meeting at 10 AM after getting no sleep. He was so tired at that meeting that he had to keep pinching himself to stay awake. And yes, he did actually stay at that Hilton once when he arrived in St. Louis late at night.

My dad was never a fan of St. Louis. Whenever I told him that I wanted to move from California to a place with less pleasant weather, he would bring up St. Louis. He told me that whenever he went there it was either really cold or really hot and humid. On some trips, he would freeze as soon as he exited the airport terminal. Though the day I was there, it was a relatively pleasant 54 degrees.

Then he said that one of the first questions people in St. Louis ask when they meet you is what high school did you go to. If you do not say a high school that they are familiar with, they don't want much to do with you, especially if you also have an accent. I told him that that is true with anywhere that people do not like you as much if you are not from there. He told me that that is not the case in California, where being from somewhere else is the norm. Some people in St. Louis did try to tell him to move there and that he could have a large piece of land or a mansion for less money than our simple tract house in L.A. But according to my dad there was a reason why these places were cheaper. He would not give up on the pleasant California weather to move somewhere like Missouri.

St. Louis is one of the cities through which Route 66 passes, and I was thinking of taking it all the way down to California. I was planning on taking a slight detour off that route to go to Branson and to Fayetteville, a liberal enclave in Arkansas that someone once suggested might be the perfect place for me to move to. However, I had been to Arkansas on the previous trip, and I could scratch Fayetteville off the list of places I might want to move to once I saw the summers there are a very humid 90 degrees. I decided to take a more northerly route through Kansas City.

I got back to St. Charles, had a breakfast of cookies from a local bakery, and then proceeded along the scenic Highway 94 that wound along the banks of the Missouri. This was the Lewis and Clark Trail, even though the explorers sailed up the actual Missouri and the river was not even visible along the vast majority of this highway. Nevertheless, the highway did wind through some beautiful countryside of forests, small towns, and some wineries. This was a good way to clear my headaches from the wireless radiation at my hotel.

The scenic highway ended just north of Jefferson City, at which point I headed to Missouri's capital. I was trying to look for the capitol building, which should have been visible above the bluffs from the fields north of the city. However, I soon noticed that the building was under repairs and encased in a cover that from a distance made it look not like a state capitol by like one of the many grain silos that dotted the landscape.

I took U.S. 50 west from Jefferson City into Kansas City. I got on the freeway right before the Kansas City suburbs started and did not now bother driving through downtown. I did not want to deal with rush hour traffic and it was getting close to sunset. Instead, I went straight to Overland Park, a large suburb where I could find a good hotel selection. I saw a very tall Sheraton from the freeway and then a Marriott. I went into the Marriott asking them for the price. It was $189, or more than $200 with taxes. I asked about the Sheraton, owned by the same corporation, and after looking it up I was told it was the same price. I asked them if there was a Residence Inn nearby, and they told me there was one two miles down. I asked them what the rate was, and they told me $119- a huge savings. I went to the Residence Inn.

I took a nap and when I woke up at 8 PM I drove out to Kansas City. Many people think Kansas City is in Kansas. Well, it is in Kansas, but the larger Kansas City is right next to it on the Missouri side of the border. I went to the downtowns of both Kansas Cities now, first to the one in Kansas because it was more on my way. Downtown Kansas City, Kansas is quite ghetto. A bleak industrial area separates it from the downtown of the one in Missouri, and that downtown is vibrant- full of tall buildings and shopping centers with lots of nightlife.

I proceeded to the corner of 18th and Vine east of downtown, where my guidebook said there would be a good Kansas City barbecue place. But first I went to 12th and Vine. This was the corner mentioned in the 1950s song "Kansas City" which still got regularly played on oldies stations when I was a child. This was one of the songs where, not understanding regional dialects, I got many of the lyrics wrong. The line "They got some crazy little women there and I'm[-a] gonna get me one" I used to think was saying "They got some crazy little women there and nothing's gonna kiss me once". The line "With my Kansas City baby and a bottle o' Kansas City wine" I used to think was "With a bottle appendix anytime", or "With a buffalo 'pendix anytime". Now when I got to 12th Street and Vine, that intersection did not exist! There was a Vine Street running perpendicular to 12th, and it might have intersected with 12th at one time, but it did not now. That stretch was now lined with apartment buildings with no streets running through them. I thought maybe this was another misheard lyric of mine and that they were saying Pine or Main instead of Vine. Also, the songwriters were 19 year olds from Los Angeles and I doubted whether they had ever been to Kansas City. I did some research and I found out that 12th Street and Vine used to be the center of Kansas City's black commercial district, but that it was cleared in the 1960s for urban renewal, with the cross streets being eliminated.

I got to 18th and Vine just after 9 PM, just missing the opening time of the barbeque place. There was a moderately upscale restaurant across the street open until 10. I went in there asking them if there were any barbecue places nearby that would still be open. They tried convincing me to get steak at their place instead. Even though the black workers and customers at that place were very inviting, I told them I still wanted the barbecue Kansas City was known for. They told me of a couple barbecue places that I could try. I went to them now. The first one was closed for the day. The second was open until 1 AM, but had a long line. I decided to go back to the steak place. There was still nearly half an hour until closing, but they told me they had already closed their kitchen. I ended up going to a hipsterish taqueria downtown. The tacos were tiny and a bit overpriced, and the place felt more L.A. than Kansas City, but the food there was very good and the meats were grass fed.

XIII. Back Out West

The following day I drove west on U.S. 56 across the state of wheat fields, sunflowers, prairie farms, Dorothy, and another girl named Lisa who went to college with me. Kansas is both an interesting and a boring place, interesting because it's Kansas, boring because, yes, there is not much to see there. It is not completely flat- there are some glacier carved hills there- but there are no dramatic elevation changes there either. One interesting aspect of Kansas is the change in scenery as one drives west across the state. In the eastern part, there are wooded areas between the farmland. A bit more arid than places farther east, but still having the form of that part of the country. Farther west, however, the scenery switches to semi-desert and there is no longer any forested country. This was now the west with its dry landscape.

I was following the old Santa Fe Trail. It was not Route 66, but something older. In the days of the wild west, this road was heavily traveled by pioneers in their wagon trains, cowboys transporting their flock, and stagecoaches. When the railroad came in, a line paralleling the wagon trail served as the main one connecting Los Angeles to Chicago and the Northeast. It is still the main rail line between these places. It is a nearly straight line from southwest to northeast that goes around the least passable parts of the Rockies. When the first transcontinental automobile highways were designated, the National Old Trails Highway connecting Los Angeles to Baltimore followed that route. However, when Route 66 followed in 1926, it took a more circuitous route into Oklahoma, a route the Interstates would later follow. This was because Cyrus Avery, the main developer of Route 66, was from Oklahoma and he wanted as much of the highway as practical to pass through his home state as to promote development there.

My stop for the night was Dodge City, the wild western town known for its outlaws and lawmen like Wyatt Earp who tried to control the place. It made perfect sense for me to stay there. Not only did this place have notorious history, it was also the only touristy town in western Kansas and the only place in the area to have a good selection of hotels. After checking in to my hotel, I went to the historic center of town hoping this would be a good tourist draw with nice shops and restaurants. What I instead found was a seedy town center that looked like the less nice parts of Oxnard. The whole town for that matter looked quite run down. But perhaps this is no surprise. In the historic period Dodge City is best known for it was not a very nice place either. It is a good thing my

Manhattan Beach friend who was born there "got the heck out of Dodge", to quote Wyatt Earp, when she did.

That evening, when I checked my Facebook, I had a message from Emily at Honeycomb telling me that everyone there was worried about me because I hadn't been there in a month. I responded that I went back to West Virginia and was sorry I did not have time to stop by before I left. The one girl whom I messaged telling her I was leaving apparently did not relay it to the others. I now realized that people in Manhattan Beach did genuinely care about me. Maybe there were incidents of people canceling on me last minute, maybe people in that place were too much tied to their dogs and smartphones, but there still were people there who cared enough to get worried when they did not see me in a month. I told Emily now that I was in the town in Kansas where Kaitlyn was born and that I would be back in Manhattan Beach in three to four days.

The following day, if I left Dodge City at 9:30, I could make it to Santa Fe and to my next hotel two hours before sunset. However, this proved easier said than done. When I left my hotel, I decided to go to the museum with Dodge City's recreated main street from the frontier days. I ended up spending half an hour walking through the complex. Then when I got on the highway, I realized I had taken the wrong road. Two versions of the Santa Fe Trail split up at Dodge City. One version cut northwest into Colorado before turning back south into New Mexico. Another version, the one I intended on taking, followed a much more direct southwesterly route to Santa Fe. I did not realize my mistake until nearly an hour after I left, when I had to detour thirty miles to get back on the southwesterly route.

The landscape here becomes increasingly desert and is quite boring. There are very few towns and the terrain is largely flat as a tabletop (though once in New Mexico things get a little bit more hilly) The elevation is rising, but the rise is imperceptible due to the flatness of the terrain and the many miles traveled for the slow rise to occur. As such, it can be a shock once one arrives at I-25 and sees the elevation is now nearly 6000 feet. To the west of I-25 are higher mountains, but the highway to Santa Fe turns south to avoid them.

Two hours before sunset I had only made it to Las Vegas- Las Vegas, New Mexico. I drove into town, the desert sun already giving me a hard time when I turned west, and made my way to the old plaza, where I parked. I walked around this colorful old Spanish town. It did not have the large hotels, casinos, and glitz of the city in Nevada, but with its boutiques and art galleries was significantly more charming. I went into the stores, now feeling well enough to do that, and told the people there that it was interesting their town was also named Las Vegas, at which they were quick to point out that their town was the original with that name. At one of the stores I asked the people if that Las Vegas was a good place to live. They told me it was. I asked them about my misgivings about New Mexico, asking them if it was correct the people there were not always that friendly (even though most of the people I met there did seem friendly, at least on the surface). They said that maybe in Albuquerque that was the case, but not in the smaller towns. Then I asked them about the high crime rate in the state. Again, they said that was Albuquerque.

I did not have something to do for two hours in this "other" Las Vegas, so with the road from there heading south, at least for the time being, I got back on the highway. Soon I was taking both the Santa Fe Trail and an old alignment of Route 66. Originally U.S. 66 turned northwest in New Mexico toward Santa Fe before turning southwest to Albuquerque, but then in 1937 it was rerouted on a less circuitous alignment bypassing Santa Fe. I had never taken the newer alignment, but this one was probably the more scenic and definitely the more historic. Soon the road turned west with the low sun still up and I did what I did in Texas the previous time. I parked on the side of the road reading my magazine, waited for the sun to dip below the mountains, then got back on the road, when I passed the mountains behind which the sun was, I again parked waiting for the sun to go all the way down, and then was able to continue.

I followed the old Santa Fe Trail straight into that town, at least the alignment known as the Old Pecos Trail. I followed the road straight to the historic part of the city, with its adobe buildings with the stores and art galleries in them and their lights still on. Soon I had arrived at the Old Spanish Plaza, having made it all the way to the end of the Santa Fe Trail.

I now went to look for parking, hoping I could go into the stores before 7 PM when most of them would likely close. I was hoping to see the friends I made at the furniture store when I visited Santa Fe last. It was right after seven when I found parking. I managed to go into one store where a Middle Eastern guy worked right at it was closing, but all the other boutiques were now closed. I went to eat at the landmark diner on the Plaza, getting a chicken bowl with cashew mole. My waitress was another friendly New Mexican, albeit one who moved there from California.

I always felt Santa Fe was a place full of magic, with its unique architecture and culture. I was sorry to only spend an hour in its historic center this time, but I had to move on. Some New Mexicans think of Santa Fe as snobby, but being someone who likes fancy things and spending time in the wealthy cities of California, this was not a problem for me. If I were to move to New Mexico, I would move to Santa Fe. Not right in the city- it still has EMFs and is a bit expensive (by New Mexico standards), but I would live somewhere close enough where I could go there whenever I wanted.

On my 2015 visit, I found out about the mining town turned hippie artists' town of Madrid twenty miles south of Santa Fe. That was where I headed the following morning. Madrid has a population of 200, comparable to that of Green Bank, and I did not see any cell towers nearby. Unlike Green Bank, however, this town is surrounded by desert mountains and its whole main street is lined with art galleries and coffeeshops. Not too many of them were open at the 9:30 AM hour I drove through town. I thought of going into the ones that were open, but skipped it when I decided it was not too unlikely there would be loose dogs inside.

I made it down to I-40 east of Albuquerque, getting off at the first exist for Route 66 after crossing into the city. The first part of Route 66/ Central Avenue was a reasonably fast road with three lanes in each direction, but farther down, one lane in each direction had recently been removed for a bus lane. Three miles from downtown the road became only one lane in each direction. I applaud the things cities are doing to encourage more public transportation. However, removing a lane of car traffic for buses or trains is not the answer. These lanes become an empty waste of space except for the few seconds when a bus or train runs through them every few minutes- 98 percent of the time they are empty. Furthermore, traffic lights are not always adjusted to account for the slower speeds when a lane is removed, thus causing long waits at the lights, as was the case on Central Avenue, and contributing to further carbon emissions by cars sitting idle longer. The mayor of Los Angeles tried removing lanes from roads a couple years prior and it was not always successful. In some neighborhoods it caused major traffic backups and it was only once the people protested that the lanes were restored. Maybe if many people continue working from home once the pandemic is over and traffic volumes remain permanently reduced, I would support the elimination of traffic lanes. These could be made into pedestrian or bike paths that are constantly used and/or greenways that add nature to the city, but let's not turn them into bus lanes that are only used for five seconds every five minutes.

I decided to check out Snowflake, Arizona, and booked a night at their bed and brreakfast. Even though it was more for Multiple Chemical Sensitives, the place was on my way. The town has an interesting history. It was settled by Mormons, who still comprise the majority of the town's population, and was founded by a Mr. Snow and Mr. Flake. Their descendants still live in town and perhaps the most famous of them was Jeff Flake, the Republican senator who resigned from the U.S. Senate after criticizing Trump. The bed and breakfast I stayed at was in a mansion that used to belong to the Flakes, but which was now owned by a couple with an Armenian last name. Unfortunately, this was one of the rare occasions where the owners were not there and I was greeted by an elderly woman who did not seem familiar with the community of sensitives. Worse, there were no phones and no public Internet at the hotel. When I arrived and found that out, I asked to cancel my stay, but the manager told me she could not do that. Finally, after settling into my room, she told me she found a way to cancel my stay. I considered, but I decided I still wanted to stay in Snowflake at that nice mansion turned hotel that used to be home to Jeff Flake's family. For the Internet, I simply went to the library. Two different friends of mine had sent me links to that day's New York Times article about Green Bank.

I drove out in the evening to the place east of town where the sensitives lived, but was not able to get in contact with anyone. The Snowflake community did not put themselves out quite as much as the Green Bank one. After seeing the latest New York Times article, I decided Green Bank was the place for me.

The following morning, I stopped at the Safeway in Holbrook along Route 66 across from the historic Wigwam Motel. This was the nearest supermarket of a large chain to Snowflake and I wanted to see what organic selection they had. Like most large mid range supermarkets, they had a decent selection.

I had been to Northern Arizona several times. In 2001, when I went with my parents, we explored all the major sites - the Petrified Forest, Meteor Crater, the Grand Canyon, Sedona, several Native American ruins. Seeing all these places, my mother decided Northern Arizona was like one large national park. I did not have time for sightseeing this time, though I did take Old Route 66 through the towns. I stopped for gas in Williams. The gas in these towns is expensive, owing to the tourism along the historic highway and to the sparseness of gas stations in these places. Gas prices in Williams were comparable to a pricey gas station in California.

Many people lament how the towns along Route 66 have died out, but that is not the case everywhere. Thanks to the attention brought to the dying towns, efforts by local businesspeople, and the popularization of the old highway in pop culture, many of these towns are thriving, and this is more the case now than twenty years ago. I remember passing through Seligman in 2001 when it was a grim town with largely abandoned storefronts. The last I was there it was full of bars, restaurants, tourist shops, and motorcyclists. That is not to say all places along Old Route 66 are still thriving. On the circuitous alignments that are now far from the freeway, the businesses are largely deserted. Even in some towns along the freeway such as Winslow, only a couple blocks by downtown are thriving and the rest of the route is composed of mostly abandoned motels.

My original plan was to get to Barstow by two hours before sunset and spend my last night there before ending my trip, or even continuing all the way back to L.A. or Oxnard if I would find something to do for two hours in Barstow and I would not be too tired. At Kingman, I got off the freeway to take a shortcut through Laughlin to avoid the part of I-40 that dips south twenty miles off course to cross the Colorado River. While Arizona Highway 68 is more direct, it is also much steeper. Over the course of ten miles, the highway drops more than 3000 feet, all along a four lane highway with not too tight curves that would be pleasant at 40 miles an hour, but not at the 55 speed limit or at the higher speeds the car is tempted to reach on the downhill. Down below, the 25 story casinos of Laughlin appear miniscule. Finally, the road reaches a couple traffic lights on the outskirts of Bullhead City. The temperature change is dramatic, having been only 70 degrees at the summit but 81 at the bottom of the valley, the hottest temperature I had on this trip so far. Soon I reached the Colorado River, forming the border with Nevada. Though this is one of the great rivers of the United States, thanks to all the dams placed on it it has much less water than the Ohio or Missouri. At Laughlin, the river appears more like a wide canal in Florida fronted by tall buildings and palm trees than it does like a grand American river.

When I got to Laughlin, I realized I would probably not make it to Barstow by two hours before sunset, so I decided to stay there instead. According to most hotel raters, the shiny high rise hotels in Laughlin are not as nice as they appear or as they were when first built around the 1980s. However, there are still a couple of good ones there, one of them being the Atlantis. I walked in to see if they had rooms, but at the registry there was a long line of at least ten minutes inside a smoke filled casino, so I decided to go elsewhere. I went back across the river to Bullhead City to look for hotels, but except for a couple cheap motels there were none. I decided to go to Lake Havasu instead. I had heard this was a beautiful place, being familiar with it as a place some friends of mine vacationed at, though I had never been there on all my trips to Arizona.

Lake Havasu took longer to reach than I expected, owing to the many traffic lights through Bullhead City. Half an hour after leaving Laughlin, but only fifteen miles away, I crossed back over the Colorado. This time, I crossed into

California. It felt good being back in my home state, but it was also not a place I so much wanted to be in. This was where my parents would try to stop me from moving to West Virginia. This was a place where the Coronavirus would likely be especially bad, owing to the many travelers between there and China. This was part of the reason why I delayed my return there. Indeed, I would not spend that night there. Twenty minutes after crossing into California to take the fast I-40, I crossed back into Arizona en route to Lake Havasu.

Each time I was crossing the river I was also crossing from Mountain Time to Pacific Time and back. Laughlin and Bullhead City might be right across from one another, but one of them is one hour ahead of the other. The following day, however, this would not be true. That was when Daylight Saving Time would begin. Since Arizona does not have Daylight Saving Time, for eight months out of the year Arizona has the same time as the places across the river and on the Pacific coast. For four months out of the year, it has the same time as the Rocky Mountain states.

Lake Havasu City is a master planned community of the 1960s that appears out of the middle of nowhere. Driving through dramatic desert rock formations, one comes upon this town of 50 000 people fronting a large lake. This is all a landscape that should not be there. There should be a free flowing river, but instead it was dammed into a large lake to provide fresh drinking water for Los Angeles. Then there is a bridge that should not be there. The London Bridge that crossed the Thames until the 1960s when its foundation began to subside was bought by the developer of Lake Havasu City and reassembled piece by piece over there so that a very English looking structure from England now sits in the middle of the Arizona desert. The bridge is not even the original construction. A new steel structure was built and the old bricks are just used as a façade. The bridge sits over a waterway that should not be there, and connecting to an island that should not be an island. Even after the lake was filled up, the ground under the London Bridge was still above water, so a trench was dug so that there could be a bridge over water. Nevertheless, the whole landscape does look beautiful. The waterfront, with its warm air and jagged mountains in the background, looks like a fancy resort found on the ocean or on a natural lake, even if this lake is not natural.

Now the problem was finding a hotel. Lake Havasu did not have as wide a selection of nice hotels as one would expect. I drove around the "island" across from London Bridge, but it was hard to tell if behind the walls of the places I was passing they were hotel resorts or housing communities. I walked into the London Bridge Hotel right across from the bridge on the "mainland", but they were nearly sold out and the cheapest room they had available went for 300 dollars. I was told the other nearby hotels were booked, it being a Saturday and Spring Break for some. I was debating whether to drive another twenty miles down to the casino on the lake, or even to wait until after sunset and just drive back to L.A. or Oxnard. I ended up going to the Nautical Resort on the "island". It was not too expensive and they had a room.

That evening, I ate at the hotel's restaurant. The beach and the building containing the restaurant and the gift shop made me feel like I was somewhere by Manhattan Beach or in Florida, but no, I was on an inland lake on the "west coast" of Arizona. I got some jalapeno poppers. Right after I started eating, someone with a large dog walked through the restaurant. I tried getting away from the dog, but the owner walked the dog toward me. That is when I said "Don't let the dog come up to me!" The waiter was asking what was going on. I said I just did not want that dog coming up to me. The person with the dog was just passing through and was soon out, but then the waiter asked me if they can call whoever was with me. I told him that I was there alone. Then he asked me if he can call my parents. I told him to stop that. I should not be treated like a mental health case just because I do not want a dog licking me.

The following day, I was ready to go back to California. I called my parents in the morning making sure they would not get mad at me for wanting to move to West Virginia and that they would still be supportive of such a move. They told me they would, but to wait until it gets warm enough for my senior parents to not freeze over there. That satisfied me.

I had run out of all my clothes, so this morning I was driving in my pajamas. I stopped at the Dillard's on the way out of Lake Havasu, but it being small town Arizona, it was not open early on Sunday. It wasn't until I got to Victorville nearly four hours later that I was able to get a shirt at a good place. That is where they have a Macy's right off the freeway and I went in there, quickly finding a short sleeve jeans shirt. I had time until sunset, and rush hour traffic would not be bad on a Sunday, so I had lunch at a Thai restaurant over there, back in a town within earshot of Los Angeles.

In Victorville I could either take highway 18 west to Oxnard or I-15 to Manhattan Beach and L.A. I went on the 15. As soon as I got to the Cajon Pass, I hit traffic. As such, I got off the freeway and took the parallel route. This was the last stretch of Old Route 66 I would take on this trip. Route 66 is not very significant past the Cajon Pass, as even in pre-Interstate days travelers had a choice of highways to take to L.A. from that point, some of which were faster than Route 66. There was U.S. 60/70/99, largely paralleling the current 60 freeway and a continuation of the U.S. highway I took intermittently from Virginia which in California has been downgraded to state highway. Those headed to the southern parts of L.A. County could take U.S. 91, which gave way to the California 91 freeway and was the road I was headed to now.

I drove down the 15 to where it intersects with the 91 in Corona. I had driven though that town many times before, but I found its name very weird now in light of the virus. On the 91, the exits were counting down 47, 46, 45. This was the number of miles left to where the highway ends a few blocks from the ocean in my favorite beach town- Manhattan Beach. I was driving down this freeway, not having any traffic and not bothered by the cell towers this time. Past the 110, the freeway ends and the route becomes the surface Artesia Boulevard. I was so happy when I saw a branch of El Pollo Inka, the Peruvian restaurant I so much liked. Driving down this familiar road with the restaurants on it that I regularly went to, I soon came upon the fancy white on blue street signs of Manhattan Beach. I was back home.

I continued down to where the road ends at the beach and to the Mexican restaurant where my friends worked. This was the restaurant where the girl who stood me up right before I went on this trip worked at. I walked by the restaurant and I thought I saw that girl working there now. I asked myself should I go in and bust her for what she did to me, or should I just not go in there. I took another look inside. It wasn't the girl who stood me up, but another waitress who looked just like her. I walked inside and this waitress asked me where had I been the past few weeks. I told her of what happened with her coworker and that I went back to West Virginia. She told me she was sorry it happened, and then I sat down with her and her busser and showed them pictures from my trip. We were all very happy to see each other. The waitress talked with the busser about some new rules for the workers. One of them I definitely liked- no cell phone use, even when the restaurant was not busy.

After showing them my pictures, I went a mile north to Downtown Manhattan Beach. I walked into Honeycomb, and everyone was very excited to see me and see that I was OK. This trip ended like all the other times I left Manhattan Beach and came back, and once again I was asking myself if I really wanted to leave that place where the people are so beautiful, the weather is so nice almost all year round, and the people seem so happy.

Then I went to my parents' for dinner. I was hoping to hug my mom after not having anyone hug me for the past month, but she did not want to do it because of Covid. I had a quick dinner with them before continuing up to Oxnard. Driving down Lincoln through Santa Monica, I reached the point that was very familiar after having driven across the country. This was where Route 66 ended, right at the intersection of Olympic Boulevard. I had passed by that junction many times before, but this time, after having driven down stretches of Route 66 from St. Louis, it was especially significant. At that intersection, a road that is now an extension of the 10 freeway, another long distance highway across the country, goes a mile farther west to the ocean and becomes Pacific Coast Highway. This was the road I took all the time to get back to Oxnard after visiting my friends.

When I got back home, I realized I did not have enough groceries, so I went to Whole Foods to get some. Even though it was fairly late at night, a time I liked to go shopping to avoid crowds, the store was fairly crowded due to panic buyers. I did not believe in that, as I thought talk of grocery stores and supply chains shutting down were just doomsdayers' predictions. After checking out, a guy on his phone stood right by me. I told him to not come toward me if he was on his phone and not to stand one foot away from me. Little did I know that a week later, phone or no phone, not standing close to others would be the norm.

Epilogue

I came back from the trip on March 8th. On March 11th, Covid-19 was declared a pandemic. I enjoyed a week of being back to my normal life before everything closed down. Stores, restaurants for dining, even the beaches, nearly every place where I enjoyed hanging out and seeing my friends. The isolation was definitely difficult, but I did my best to cope. I did the things I enjoyed doing and which I was still allowed. I regularly went on two hour drives, which was a good way to break the monotony of quarantining. Sometimes I would drive to the Manhattan Beach area to the four branches of the Mexican restaurant where I could still talk to my friends at the front window. Mostly I just sat at home by my computer doing various things, such as researching the songs that have been number one in different countries and building Youtube playlists of them.

Moving to West Virginia was not practical now. Even if I could sell my house and manage to drive across the country during lockdown, I would arrive at a very isolated place. Even as things started opening up in May, the Green Bank Observatory remained closed to visitors and all the public areas of the hotel where I stayed remained closed with guests being checked in with no contact. In other words, a place that was fairly isolated before the pandemic now offered almost no opportunities for socializing.

Despite the difficulties in travel during the pandemic, however, I went on four more overnight trips before 2020 was over. Not having the things I was used to in California sometimes meant going to other states to have them. I was also looking at other places to move to temporarily that might offer more social opportunities than Green Bank. If cell phone radiation was low enough, the people were kind enough, and the place was better than West Virginia, I might stay there permanently. I considered places such as Utah and North Dakota, but I was glad I did not move there once they had major Covid surges.

Maybe I did not need to leave California to find less radiation. Even if more people were working from home and using more Internet and phone bandwidth, fewer people in public places meant fewer cell phones. And where people were in public, it seemed that they were using their devices less, as they now had a greater appreciation for real life experiences. Fewer cars on the road meant less air pollution, another contributor to my radiation symptoms. As a result, I no longer had a migraine nearly every day. When Downtown Ventura reopened its stores and restaurants and I went strolling there one evening, I did not have as many cell phones to evade as I had dogs.

Not everyone was willing to hang out, even as things reopened, but when they did not, I knew it was because of Covid and not because I was not someone they wanted to hang out with. Stasia would not go to restaurants until she would get the vaccine, but she did occasionally come to my house where we hung out in my front yard at least six feet apart. Monica did stand me up a few more times, but one time we actually did get dinner. Right in the middle of the lockdown we got takeout sushi and ate it on a table at the plaza in Downtown Manhattan Beach. I soon found a couple friends on whom I could rely not to cancel on me, including Marie, who was back from Texas once she graduated. Maybe my friends did not always have time due to their busy schedules, but when we did meet up we had a good time. And my friends at the stores seemed a bit kinder, even if we could not see our full faces behind the masks.

I was now undecided as whether to stay in California or leave. The restrictions in the state were too tight and restrictions that might have been necessary at the height of the pandemic I was not sure how long they would last. I did not want us to lose our ability to read faces due to prolonged mandatory mask wearing. I did not want to be in a place where there would be a whole generation who never adequately learned how to interact in person with others because they did not have in person school for more than a year, and where they and other members of society would become more used to interacting by screen than in person. Other states would ease their restrictions sooner, as was already the case with schools and other things, but that would not happen in California, not with the ones running the state.

California was still an expensive place. People were still tied to their cell phones there, and I knew once the pandemic would be over the streets would again be filled with people on them. More people got dogs during the pandemic, and they would likely not give up on them once everything was over, so I did not know how crowded public places would be with the hounds when the number of people there would return to normal. My neighbors' dogs were still very loud and often prevented me from getting an adequate amount of sleep. I sold my house in January 2021 not sure where I wanted to end up. My heart is in Manhattan Beach, California. My heart is in Green Bank, West Virginia. My heart is also in Ohio where some friends of mine who have also left California have relocated.

I very much hope the pandemic will be a wake up call that we need better standards for society. We need to have health standards that are not decided by large corporations that are more interested in profits than the good of the people, not decided by pessimistic conspiracy theorists, but by hard science. We need to have fairly conducted scientific studies on radiation from wireless devices that are not skewed in favor of the phone and tech industries or in favor of rogue academics who want to earn brownie points by claiming they discovered something. We already have some fairly conducted studies and while they do not show wireless radiation will kill off millions of people they do not show it is completely harmless.

This is not to say we should get rid of all cell phones and wireless technology. Our society is too dependent on them and they also provide a great good even if they give out some radiation. Rather, we should make some modifications. We should acknowledge the potential for harm from the radiation and develop ALARA (as low as reasonably achievable) standards for the radiation output both from the devices and in the environment. We should develop wireless technology using electromagnetic waves such as infrared and visible light that are already present in the environment in large amounts and to which humans and all life living on the earth's surface are adapted to, unlike the microwaves current technology uses and which are virtually nonexistent in the natural environment. We need to invest more in wired technology. We need to lay down more fiber optic cables to serve technologically underserved communities, not more 4G and 5G towers or satellites in space. We need to use wired technology whenever feasible.

We need to develop more flexible wired connectivity, such as by making all Internet ready devices be able to connect through a simple USB cable with ports that will be as ubiquitous someday as wi-fi is now. These ports can easily be installed in public spaces, restaurants, trains, and even airplanes. The devices will still have wireless capabilities for when using a cable is not feasible, but where one is stationary somewhere and next to a USB outlet, one will easily be able to have a radiation free wired connection. Where this system will be placed on public transportation, wireless will of course need to be used to connect the vehicle to the phones and Internet, but people will be exposed to much less radiation. There will only be one antenna used for connection rather than one antenna for each of the many devices in the vehicle. The connection point will be outside the body of the vehicle, thus eliminating the Faraday Cage effect where the radiation gets amplified inside the metallic structure. Furthermore, those who are more sensitive to the radiation will be able to sit farther from the external antenna. If airplanes will start using this system instead of wi-fi, I will fly again.

To be continued…

Made in the USA
Las Vegas, NV
13 January 2024

84232120R00095